TOPICS AND LANGUAGE COMPETENCIES

6

MICHAEL KERWIN

SERIES ADVISOR — LEANN HOWARD

PRENTICE HALL REGENTS

Publisher: Mary Jane Peluso
Editor: Sheryl Olinsky
Development Editor: Janet Johnston
Production Editor/Compositor: Paula D. Williams
Interior Design and Electronic Art: Ken Liao
Manufacturing Manager: Ray Keating
Art Director: Merle Krumper
Cover Design: Pakhaus

PRENTICE HALL REGENTS

Printed in the United States of America

10   9   8   7   6   5

ISBN 0-13-435918-6

• • • • • • • • • • • **CONTENTS** • • • • • • • • • • •

UNIT 1: ON THE JOB

UNIT 2: RECREATION AND LEISURE ACTIVITIES

UNIT 3: ON WRITING

UNIT 4: DEMOCRATIC GOVERNMENT

UNIT 5: TECHNOLOGY

To my wife, Terry. Thank you again for your love, help, and patience.

ACKNOWLEDGMENTS

This series would have never gotten off the ground without the help and encouragement of the Prentice Hall Regents specialists in California, especially Gordon Johnson, Tom Dare, and Eric Bredenberg.

To Nancy Baxer, my editor, whose encouragement, insights, and hard work brought this series to the printer.

To Leann Howard, for her valuable comments and direction.

To Janet Johnston, whose contributions, continuous effort, experience, expertise, and editiorial skills contributed immensely.

To Sheryl Olinsky, who was with this project from the start, took over in the middle, and never dropped the ball.

To Ken Liao, for his design and occasional illustrations.

To Wanda España, Marita Froimson, Nicole Cypher, and Paula Williams for the realia.

To my fellow teachers and friends at the Centre de Linguistique Appliquée, Besançon, France, where it all began for me.

To all of my students throughout the world, who taught me more than they will ever know.

To Shayne West, Rad Davis, Dean Cooper, Toby Phillips, Michael Faber, and Einstein Studios for audio and music development and production.

To Nancy Minard and the Verona (New Jersey) Free Public Library for the library card catalog material.

To Bayard W. Johnston, programmer, Comm-Tech Associates, for information on computer programming language and procedures.

To my family, who have given me the time and the space to work.

To Terry Kerwin, for her endless hours of help in the development and preparation of the text, and audio development and production.

Thank you one and all.

INTRODUCTION

Topics and Language Competencies (TLC) 6 is designed for young adult and adult ESL/ESOL students at the advanced-high level of ESL instruction, SPL (MELT) level 5–6, CASAS ESL proficiency level C (216 +), and California ESL adult education level advanced high. *TLC* covers the topics, language skills, functions, and forms established by the California English as a Second Language Model Standards for Adult Education and the CASAS ESL Competencies. *TLC* can be used alone or as a supplemental text with existing basal ESL/ESOL series to bring real-life topics, situations, skills, and materials to the classroom.

TLC 6 is designed for students who have had increased exposure to English. It provides these students with topics, language functions, and language forms they need to communicate successfully. These language functions and forms are integrated with informational sources, skills, and topics that are relevant to the students' general and vocational goals. Each unit contains illustrations and realia that aid student comprehension. In addition, the <u>cassette tapes</u> provide the students with realistic language as it is used outside the classroom. <u>Teacher's guides</u> are available to provide both less experienced and master teachers with a variety of ideas on how to use the material meaningfully in the classroom.

In each unit, *TLC* integrates all of the four language skills — listening/speaking, grammar, reading, and writing. Picture pages give the students a visual representation of vocabulary, people, places, and objects they will encounter throughout the book. <u>Scenes</u> feature realistic conversations that the students hear on the cassette, followed by selective listening tasks and practices. <u>Practices</u> give the students a chance to work with realia, such as forms and applications, similar to those they will encounter outside the classroom. Pair and group work activities give the students the opportunity to have fun with language and use it creatively. <u>Lifeskills/Workskills</u> present the students with content relevant to their personal and vocational goals. <u>Cross-Cultural Discussions</u> allow the students to discuss aspects of their own cultures, such as educational systems, and to compare and contrast them to aspects of U.S. culture. <u>Supplemental Activities</u> provide additional opportunities for students to learn about, ask for, and receive social and factual information. In the <u>Summary</u>, the students check off the functions, forms, and topics learned in the unit.

TO THE TEACHER

Icons are used throughout *TLC* to indicate to you and your students what type of activity follows. Here are suggestions on how to use the material.

 Play the tape. After the first listening, ask the students questions so they know what to listen for as you play the tape the second time. Possible questions are "Where is the scene taking place?" "Who are the characters?" "What are the characters doing?" Go over the directions for the listening task. Play the tape again and have the students complete the listening task. Correct and evaluate their work individually, or go over it with the whole class.

 Either have the students cover the dialogue in their books and listen to the conversation on the tape, or have them follow along with the book while they are listening to the tape.

Tasks with this icon check students' comprehension and ability to express themselves in writing. You may want to model or demonstrate individual exercises on the board. Have the students complete the task in their books. Then correct and evaluate their work individually, or go over the task with the whole class.

Tasks with this icon have students interact with each other in English to practice various language skills and tasks in different situations. Start by modeling each exercise for the class. Assign each student a partner and give the partners a time frame to complete the exercise. Be sure to give each pair enough time to complete the task and then change roles. Walk around the classroom to observe, encourage, and provide assistance to each of the pairs. When all the pairs have finished, ask a few of them to perform their work for the rest of the class.

Activities with this icon are group discussion tasks. Explain and describe the task or topic and the procedures for participating. Set a time frame. Then ask for a volunteer from each group to be the discussion leader for the group. If no one volunteers, appoint a discussion leader. Encourage all students to participate in their groups. If necessary, get involved with groups yourself to promote more conversation. Ask for a volunteer student to summarize the group's findings and to present the findings to the class.

Information with this icon is optional and is included as a reference for students and teachers. Although the information may be somewhat difficult for some students, others may find it a stimulating challenge.

Unit 1 On the Job

TOPICS

- ▲ Business letters
- ▲ Letters of application
- ▲ Resumés
- ▲ Job promotion strategies
- ▲ Problems on the job
- ▲ Job evaluations/Reviews
- ▲ Memo

LANGUAGE FUNCTIONS

On completion, students will have used English for:

- ▲ factual information: to analyze, to evaluate, to paraphrase, to summarize.
- ▲ social and interpersonal relations: to express values, to express judgement.
- ▲ suasion: to compromise, to negotiate, to bargain.

LANGUAGE FORMS

On completion, students will have used the following structures:

- ▲ **Sentence types**
  Complex sentences
  Noun clauses
  Tag questions

LANGUAGE SKILLS

Listening: On completion, students will have:

- ▲ demonstrated understanding of conversation in encounters with native speakers with little repetition or rewording.
- ▲ demonstrated understanding of descriptions and narrations of factual and technical material.

Speaking: On completion, students will have:

- ▲ spoken fluently in most formal and informal conversations on practical and social topics, except when under tension or pressure.
- ▲ spoken with some fluency on technical subjects or on special fields of interest related to academic pursuits or work demands.

Reading: On completion, students will have:

- ▲ read authentic printed material and prose on familiar topics.
- ▲ read short stories and other recreational literature.
- ▲ interpreted main ideas and key points in technical material in their own fields of interest.
- ▲ applied appropriate reading strategies for understanding content on unfamiliar topics or in technical information.
- ▲ used syntactic clues to interpret the meaning of complex sentences and new vocabulary.

Writing: On completion, students will have:

- ▲ punctuated paragraphs, making only minor errors.
- ▲ taken notes from lectures.
- ▲ written simple outlines of reading passages and lectures.
- ▲ written summaries of reading passages.
- ▲ written letters to accompany job applications.

A Business-Letter Format

Scene 1

Topic: A business letter

(name) _____   sender's information

_____
(street address)

_____
(city, state, zip code)

_____
(phone or FAX #)

_____   date

(receiver's name) _____   receiver's information

_____
(street address)

_____
(city, state, zip code)

Dear _____ :
(salutation or attention line: Dear Mr., Mrs., Miss, Ms., Attention, etc.)

(State the reason for the letter. Be clear and concise.)

_____

_____   body of letter

_____

_____

(Paragraph 2: Expand on the reason for the letter.)

_____

_____

_____

_____

_____ ,   complimentary closing
(Yours truly, Sincerely yours, etc.)

_____   handwritten signature

_____   typewritten signature

_____   title of sender, if appropriate

Writing a Business Letter

Topics: Business letters, writing a letter

Use the business-letter format to write to one of the companies listed. Explain that you have a problem with a product they produce. Then check your work with a partner.

Partner's name _____

Acme Manufacturing
1415 E. Main St.
Los Angeles, CA 92010

Best Sporting Goods
32 Pacific Drive
San Diego, CA

_____

_____

_____

_____

_____

_____

_____

_____

_____

_____

_____

_____

_____

_____

_____

_____

_____

_____

_____

_____

_____

_____

Scene 2

A Letter of Application

Topics: Letters of application, the business-letter format

Gerry Protheroe
1616 Adams Ave.
Anaheim, CA 92804
March 3, 1997

Mr. Howard Burns
Best Products
80 West End Drive
Los Angeles, CA 90211

Dear Mr. Burns:

    I would like to introduce myself and apply for the sales position advertised in the *Herald* on March 1, 1997.

    I am currently working in sales for Ace Manufacturing. I have been with Ace for two years, and I am now the assistant sales manager. I graduated in 1994 from Anaheim Community College with an Associate of Arts degree in marketing.

    Please feel free to contact me by phone at (714) 555-1347 with any questions or to arrange an interview. Thank you for your consideration. I look forward to hearing from you.

                  Sincerely,
                  Gerry Protheroe

Practice 2

Writing a Letter of Application

Topics: Letters of application, the business-letter format

In the classified section of a local newspaper, find a job notice that interests you. On page 5 write a letter of application, using the business-letter format above.

Remember to include:
    in the 1st paragraph,
- the job you are interested in
- where you heard or read about the job

    in the 2nd and 3rd paragraph(s),
- your qualifications for the job
- your present position
- your previous experience and education

    in the last paragraph,
- a request for an interview
- a thank-you for their consideration
- information about how to contact you.

Writing a Letter of Application
(continued)

Topics: Letters of application, the business-letter format

_____

_____

_____

_____

_____

_____

_____

_____

_____

_____

_____

_____

_____

_____

_____

_____

_____

_____

_____

_____

_____

_____

_____

_____

_____

_____

_____

_____

_____

_____

_____

_____

_____

Contents of a Resumé

Topics: Resumés, note-taking

Scene 3

Listen to the lecture on resumés.

I. Types of resumés
- Chronological: presents a general picture of applicant's experience, background, and education in reverse order, starting with the most recent.
- Functional: presents applicant's assets, with the most important first.

II. Content of Resumé
- Personal information: your name, address, and phone number at the top of your resumé
- Employment objective: complete sentences describing the kind of position you are looking for and why you are the best candidate for the position
- Employment history: complete sentences listing your most recent employer, his address, your position or job title, and your responsibilities. Add remaining job history in backwards order.
- Educational background: the name and location of the schools you attended. Include the dates attended and/or graduated, your major, and the type of diploma, degree, or certificate you received.
- Special interests or skills: remember to include computer skills, language skills, or other job-related skills not mentioned elsewhere.
- References: a list of three or four people who can comment on you personally. These could be former employers, teachers, or other community leaders. Include their names, addresses, telephone numbers, and job titles if appropriate.

III. Update your resumé at regular intervals.

Taking Notes at a Lecture

Topics: Note-taking, resumés, listening to a lecture

Listen to Scene 3 again and take notes. Then compare your notes with a partner's. Did you include all the important information? Add any that you missed.

Partner's name _____

Notes: _____

_____

_____

_____

_____

_____

_____

_____

_____

_____

_____

_____

_____

_____

_____

_____

_____

_____

_____

_____

_____

_____

_____

_____

_____

Harry Protheroe's Resumé

Topic: A brief resumé

Note all the components of this resumé.

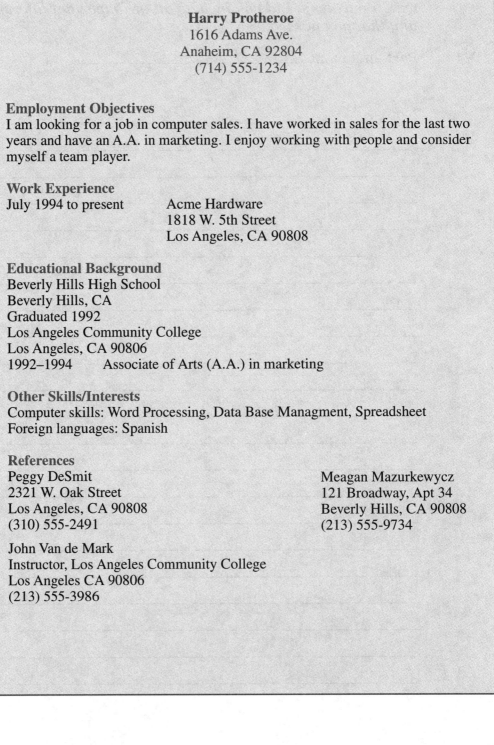

Harry Protheroe
1616 Adams Ave.
Anaheim, CA 92804
(714) 555-1234

Employment Objectives
I am looking for a job in computer sales. I have worked in sales for the last two years and have an A.A. in marketing. I enjoy working with people and consider myself a team player.

Work Experience
July 1994 to present   Acme Hardware
                            1818 W. 5th Street
                            Los Angeles, CA 90808

Educational Background
Beverly Hills High School
Beverly Hills, CA
Graduated 1992
Los Angeles Community College
Los Angeles, CA 90806
1992–1994   Associate of Arts (A.A.) in marketing

Other Skills/Interests
Computer skills: Word Processing, Data Base Managment, Spreadsheet
Foreign languages: Spanish

References
Peggy DeSmit   Meagan Mazurkewycz
2321 W. Oak Street   121 Broadway, Apt 34
Los Angeles, CA 90808   Beverly Hills, CA 90808
(310) 555-2491   (213) 555-9734

John Van de Mark
Instructor, Los Angeles Community College
Los Angeles CA 90806
(213) 555-3986

Name _____   **Date** _____

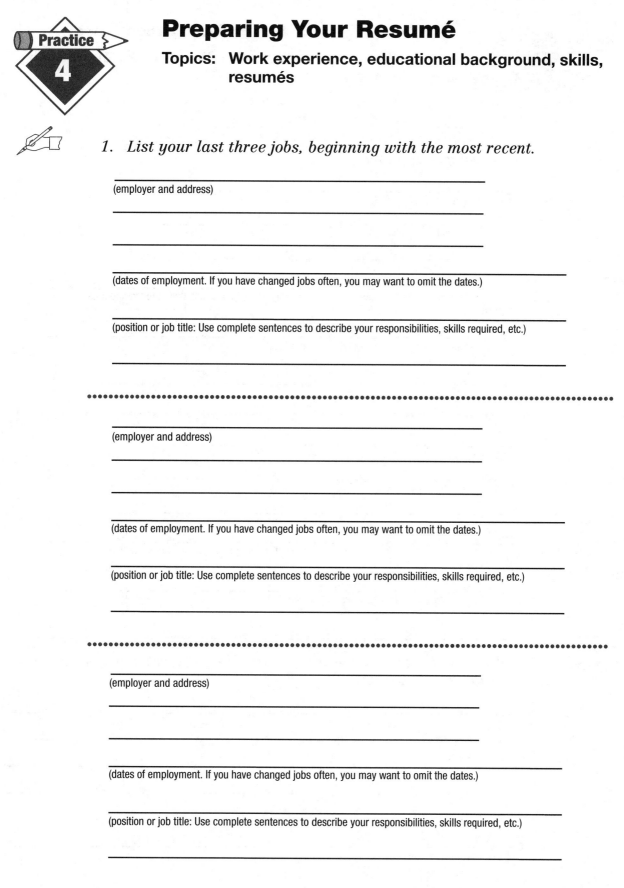

Preparing Your Resumé

Topics: Work experience, educational background, skills, resumés

1. *List your last three jobs, beginning with the most recent.*

_____

(employer and address)

_____

_____

_____

(dates of employment. If you have changed jobs often, you may want to omit the dates.)

_____

(position or job title: Use complete sentences to describe your responsibilities, skills required, etc.)

_____

• •

_____

(employer and address)

_____

_____

_____

(dates of employment. If you have changed jobs often, you may want to omit the dates.)

_____

(position or job title: Use complete sentences to describe your responsibilities, skills required, etc.)

_____

• •

_____

(employer and address)

_____

_____

_____

(dates of employment. If you have changed jobs often, you may want to omit the dates.)

_____

(position or job title: Use complete sentences to describe your responsibilities, skills required, etc.)

_____

Preparing Your Resumé (continued)

Topics: Work experience, educational background, skills, resumés

2. *List your educational background, beginning with the most recent school you attended.*

_____
(school name)

_____
(address: city and state only)

_____

_____
(dates of attendance or graduation. If you are attending school at present, write the starting date and "to present.")

_____
(major studied, diploma, degree, or certificate received)

_____

• •

_____
(school name)

_____
(address: city and state only)

_____

_____
(dates of attendance or graduation. If you are attending school at present, write the starting date and "to present.")

_____
(major studied, diploma, degree, or certificate received)

_____

3. *Other skills. List any other special training, work skills, language skills, computer skills, etc.*

_____

_____

_____

_____

_____

_____

Putting It All Together

Topic: Preparing a resumé

Complete this resumé form with your information.

_____

_____

_____

_____

Employment objectives

_____

_____

_____

Employment history

_____

_____

_____

_____

_____

_____

_____

_____

_____

_____

_____

_____

_____

_____

_____

Practice 5

Putting It All Together (continued)

Topic: Preparing a resumé

Educational background

_____

_____

_____

_____

_____

_____

_____

_____

Other training, skills, interests

_____

_____

_____

_____

References

_____   _____

_____   _____

_____   _____

_____   _____

_____   _____

_____   _____

_____   _____

Job Review

Topics: Job evaluations, job-promotion strategy

Read over Serge's Job Performance Review.

EMPLOYEE JOB PERFORMANCE REVIEW

Employee: Serge Valencia

Using the following scale, rate your performance over the past six months in each of categories listed. If you would like to include a brief description, space is provided.

> 4 = Outstanding performance: consistently exceeds job requirements.
> 3 = Above-average performance: usually performs above acceptable standards and job requirements.
> 2 = Average performance: meets job standards and requirements.
> 1 = Below-average performance: needs improvement.
> 0 = Unacceptable perrformance: fails to meet position standards. Immediate improvement is required.

After completing, submit your form to your supervisor. He or she will complete his/her parts and comments and schedule an appointment for a review of the evaluation.

PART A: Evaluation Ratings (circle one)

	Employee	Supervisor
Attendance and punctuality	0 1 2 3 ④	0 1 2 ③ 4
Professional appearance	0 1 2 3 ④	0 ① 2 3 4
Timely and efficient organization of work	0 1 2 3 ④	0 1 ② 3 4
Operates through channels	0 1 2 3 ④	0 1 2 ③ 4
Works diligently to accomplish tasks	0 1 2 3 ④	0 1 ② 3 4
Demonstrates initiative	0 1 2 3 ④	0 1 ② 3 4
Attitude	0 1 2 3 ④	0 1 2 ③ 4

Employee's comments: *I like my job, and everybody likes me. I think I should get a promotion.*

Supervisor's comments: *Serge is a hard worker. He needs to spend more time working and less time talking with other employees. He also should spend more time learning about the job and improving his skills.*

Scene 5

Job Review (continued)

Topics: Job evaluations, job-promotion strategy

PART B: Accomplishments and Growth

1. Describe any professional development you have had in the last six months. (Include classes attended, training received, OJT, computer skills, etc.)

   None _____

   _____

2. Describe or list any positive contributions you have made to the company/organization in the last six months.

   _____

   _____

   _____

3. Describe or list what you would like to accomplish for the company/organization in the next six months.

   _____

   _____

   _____

Employee's comments: *I've worked for this company for 8 months, and I've only gotten 1 raise. I would like a raise and a promotion.*

Supervisor's comments: *Serge is a good employee, but has not demonstrated any initiative to improve his knowledge of the job. He is rarely late for work, but does not dress in a professional manner.*

Each employee is required to sign this form to acknowledge that he or she has participated in the evaluation process and has read this rating form. Your signature does not mean that you agree with the rating but merely that you have read it.

Employee's comments (optional) _____

Employee's signature: *Serge Valencia*   **Date:** *4/02/96*

Reviewer's signature: *Lin Phan*   **Date:** *4/02/96*

Read over Serge's performance review with a partner. Then suggest some things Serge can do or change to get a better review next time and the promotion and raise he wants.   Partners name _____

_____

_____

Name _____   Date _____

Satish Arrived Late for Work Again!
Topic: Problems at work

*Read about the situations at work. You are the manager of a
small company. With a small group, decide how you would
respond to each situation and why. Have one person take notes
and report your group's comments to the class.*

Group reporter: _____

Situation 1. Satish arrived late for work again! This is the third time in two
weeks. He's a good worker, but he doesn't think it is important to be on time.

_____

_____

_____

Situation 2. Lin, a single parent, works well with other employees and
always arrives early for work. Recently her daughter has been very sick, but
she hasn't missed any work or even been late. You noticed that she has been
crying a lot at work because she is worried about her daughter.

_____

_____

_____

Situation 3. Bill is constantly complaining about his job and the people he
works with. This disrupts work and is not good for morale.

_____

_____

_____

Situation 4. Maria speaks very little English. She has trouble understanding
her supervisor. Today she almost got hurt because she didn't understand her
supervisor.

_____

_____

_____

Situation 5. Marco needs a raise, but he just received a raise last month.
Salaries are reviewed every six months, but Marco is your best employee,
and you don't want to lose him.

_____

_____

Communicating About Problem Situations

Topics: Communication styles, body language

Work with a partner. Use the situation to write a dialogue. After writing and practicing the scene, present your scene to the class. Your scene should be at least a minute long.

Partner's name _____

Situation: I Should Have Gotten Your Job!

Characters: Employee A and supervisor

Employee A: You have had the same job for five years. During that time you have been a model employee, as well as Employee of the Month six times. You are always on time for work and work any overtime that is needed. In five years you have not missed a day of work.

The company just hired a new supervisor for your department. Your fellow employees thought you would be promoted to the position, but you were not.

Supervisor: You just finished college and have no previous work experience. This is your first week on the job, the tension is thick, and you don't know why. You must do something about it right away. You decide to talk to Employee A because she/he seems to be the most knowledgeable about the department and the other employees.

_____

_____

_____

_____

_____

_____

_____

_____

_____

_____

Cross-Cultural
Discussion
1

Communicating at Work

Topics: Communication styles, body language

Work in a small group of three to five people. Have one person take notes and present your group's comments to the class.

Group reporter: _____

1. Have you ever had trouble communicating at work? Explain.

    _____

    _____

2. Have you ever had trouble communicating with your supervisor? Explain.

    _____

    _____

3. Have you ever had trouble communicating with a fellow employee? Explain.

    _____

    _____

4. Have you ever had trouble communicating at work in an emergency? Explain.

    _____

    _____

5. Is it important to understand the communication style of your supervisor? Explain why.

    _____

    _____

6. Is it important to understand the body language (eye contact, facial expressions, gestures, etc.) of the person you are speaking with? Explain why.

    _____

    _____

7. Do different cultures interpret body language in different ways? Give an example.

    _____

    _____

Supplemental Activity 1

Tag Questions

Topics: Grammar skills, tag questions

Tag questions are questions added to the end of a sentence. They are used to check or clarify information, and to show agreement. We usually use rising intonation on the tag question when we want to check or clarify information.

Example: You are studying with a group. You don't know what page everyone is working on. You might ask:

We're working on page 101, aren't we? *(with rising intonation)*

We use falling intonation when we think the listener agrees with us.

Example: You and your co-worker think that you can complete a project by 4 o'clock. Your boss is not so sure, and you want to assure him. You might ask your co-worker:

We can finish this by 4, can't we? *(with falling intonation)*

Add a tag question to each sentence. Then work with a partner and practice saying the tag questions with rising and falling intonation. Do they change the meaning of the sentences? Describe the difference, if any.

Partner's name: _____

1. I ordered the fish, _____?
   Meaning
   with falling intonation: _____
   with rising intonation: _____

2. We want to go to the seminar, _____?
   Meaning
   with falling intonation: _____
   with rising intonation: _____

3. She's the best employee you have, _____?
   Meaning
   with falling intonation: _____
   with rising intonation: _____

4. We should practice speaking English all the time, _____?
   Meaning
   with falling intonation: _____
   with rising intonation: _____

5. That restaurant serves Mexican food, _____?
   Meaning
   with falling intonation: _____
   with rising intonation: _____

Summary: On the Job Checklist

Check (✓) one.

Yes   No   Need more practice

☐ ☐ ☐ I can write a business letter in a business-letter format. (example: p. 2. *"State the reason for the letter."*)

☐ ☐ ☐ I can write a letter of application. (example: p. 4–5. *"I would like to introduce myself."*)

☐ ☐ ☐ I can write a resumé. (example: p. 11–12)

☐ ☐ ☐ I can talk about job-promotion strategies. (example: p. 13 or 14, or both)

☐ ☐ ☐ I can talk about problems at work. (example: p. 15. *"Satish arrived late for work again!"*)

☐ ☐ ☐ I can talk about communication problems at work. (example: p. 17. *"It is important to understand body language."*)

Write two other things you can say or do in English.

I can _____.

I can _____.

_____
Signature

Teacher's comments: _____

_____

Unit 2 Recreation and Leisure Activities

TOPICS

- ▲ Recreation
- ▲ Entertainment
- ▲ Television
- ▲ Oral presentations
- ▲ Writing paragraphs
- ▲ Public health facilities and services
- ▲ Weddings

LANGUAGE FUNCTIONS

On completion, students will have used English for:

- ▲ factual information: to analyze, to evaluate, to paraphrase, to summarize.
- ▲ social and interpersonal relations: to express values, to express judgment.

LANGUAGE FORMS

On completion, students will have used the following structures:

- ▲ **Sentence types**
  Complex sentences
  Subjunctive sentences
  Noun clauses

LANGUAGE SKILLS

Listening: On completion, students will have:

- ▲ demonstrated understanding of descriptions and narrations of factual and technical material.

Speaking: On completion, students will have:

- ▲ spoken fluently in most formal and informal conversations on practical and social topics, except when under tension or pressure.
- ▲ demonstrated control of grammatical patterns—including perfect tenses, passive constructions, complex sentences, and the conditional tense—although with some hesitation when choosing accurate grammar and appropriate vocabulary.

Reading: On completion, students will have:

- ▲ read authentic printed material and prose on familiar topics.
- ▲ applied appropriate reading strategies for understanding content on unfamiliar topics or in technical information.
- ▲ used syntactic clues to interpret the meaning of complex sentences and new vocabulary.
- ▲ reacted to reading materials by making personal judgments or by prioritizing values.

Writing: On completion, students will have:

- ▲ punctuated paragraphs, making only minor errors.
- ▲ written paragraphs on familiar topics, using the techniques of comparison/contrast, cause/effect, generalization/example, and exposition.
- ▲ written summaries of reading passages.

Favorite Recreations and Leisure Activities

Scene 7

Topics: Types of recreation, interviewing, and collecting information

Interview a classmate about his or her favorite recreation or leisure activity. It might be one of the activities pictured or something entirely different. Ask as many questions as you can think of so you can learn all about the activity.

Classmate's name _____

Include these questions.

Favorite activity or recreation:_____

Where does it take place? _____

Does it take place during certain seasons of the year? If so, which?

_____

How often do you do the activity? _____

Do you need special equipment or clothing? If so, what? _____

How long have you been doing this activity? _____

Did you do this activity in your home country? _____

Did you need special training?_____

Other information _____

_____

_____

Practice 7

Describing Recreations and Leisure Activities

Topics: Writing a report, constructing paragraphs

You are going to write a report. You may report what you learned from the classmate you interviewed for page 22, or you may interview another classmate and write a report on his or her favorite recreation or leisure activity. Use the same types of questions you asked on page 2 to learn as much information as possible about your classmate's activity. Then write a report of several paragraphs, using complete sentences. Check your punctuation. Do not include your classmate's name.

Have your teacher look over and comment on what you have written. Rewrite your paragraph if needed, making any corrections your teacher suggests. Can your class recognize whose favorite recreation or leisure activity you have written about?

_____
_____
_____
_____
_____
_____
_____
_____

Rewrite if necessary.

_____
_____
_____
_____
_____
_____
_____
_____
_____

My Favorite Leisure Activity Is _____.

Scene 8

Topics: Oral presentations, preparing and giving an oral report

You have interviewed a classmate about his or her preferred recreation or leisure activity. Now you will write a report on a recreation or leisure activity (such as a sport or music) that you like. First make notes to answer these questions.

1. What is the recreation called?

2. When and how did you become interested in or start participating in the activity?

3. Write a short general description of the activity and how it is done.

4. Where does this type of recreation or activity usually take place (in the mountains, on a field, in a pool, in your living room)?

5. Do you need any special equipment or clothing?

6. Do you need any special skills, training, or physical aptitude for this type of activity? Describe.

7. Explain why you like it.

8. How can others find out more about this kind of recreation?

_____

_____

_____

_____

_____

_____

_____

Now form your notes into a written report, using complete sentences. Give your report to the class as an oral presentation lasting at least three minutes. Bring to class any pictures or special equipment (and perhaps demonstrate its use) that might help you in your presentation. When you have finished, ask the class if they have any questions; answer them.

How many other people in the class have done this activity before? How many would like to try? If you have persuaded anyone that he or she would like to try the activity, you have given an interesting presentation!

**Practice
8**

Evaluating Oral Presentations

Topics: Listening to and evaluating oral presentations,
figuring averages

An EVALUATION *is a means of recording your judgment of something
and of comparing two or more of the same things. Use these forms to
evaluate three classmates' presentations.*

ORAL PRESENTATION EVALUATION

Presenter's name _____   Topic/Title _____

1 = Poor	2 = Needs work	3 = Good	4 = Excellent

Circle one:

Pronunciation (easy to understand)	1	2	3	4
Fluency (easy to follow)	1	2	3	4
Preparation (well thought-out)	1	2	3	4
Overall presentation	1	2	3	4

Total score (add all the scores)   _____
Average score (total score divided by 4)   _____
Other comments _____

_____

ORAL PRESENTATION EVALUATION

Presenter's name _____   Topic/Title _____

1 = Poor	2 = Needs work	3 = Good	4 = Excellent

Circle one:

Pronunciation (easy to understand)	1	2	3	4
Fluency (easy to follow)	1	2	3	4
Preparation (well thought-out)	1	2	3	4
Overall presentation	1	2	3	4

Total score (add all the scores)   _____
Average score (total score divided by 4)   _____
Other comments _____

_____

ORAL PRESENTATION EVALUATION

Presenter's name _____   Topic/Title _____

1 = Poor	2 = Needs work	3 = Good	4 = Excellent

Circle one:

Pronunciation (easy to understand)	1	2	3	4
Fluency (easy to follow)	1	2	3	4
Preparation (well thought-out)	1	2	3	4
Overall presentation	1	2	3	4

Total score (add all the scores)   _____
Average score (total score divided by 4)   _____
Other comments _____

_____

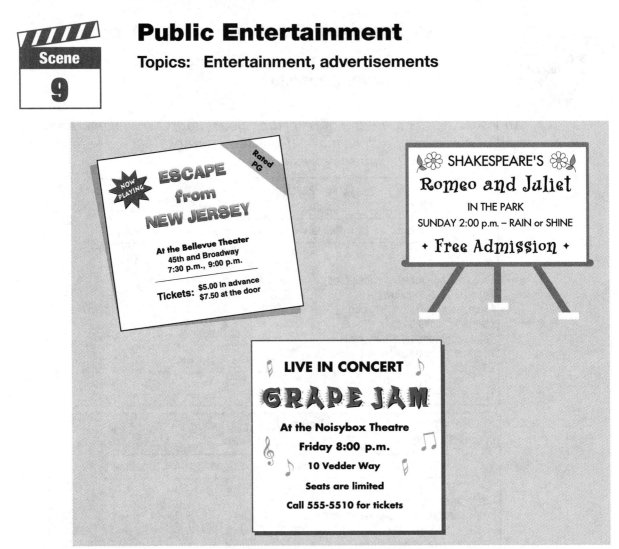

Public Entertainment

Topics: Entertainment, advertisements

 With your class, discuss the advertisements for the entertainment events shown in the illustrations. Pick one to write about. Include its name, the kind of event (play, movie, concert), where and when the event takes place, where to get tickets, and their cost. Add any other information you can find on the poster. Use complete sentences.

1. _____

    _____

2. _____

    _____

3. _____

    _____

Defining Types of Public Entertainment

Topics: Using resources, writing definitions

Use a dictionary or other reference source to find the meanings of the words. Write a short definition for each word. Then use the entertainment section of a local newspaper to find an example for each form of entertainment. Compare your answers with a partner's.

Partner's name _____

1. **Fiction** Example: _____

    Definition: _____

2. **Nonfiction** Example: _____

    Definition: _____

3. **A play** Example: _____

    Definition: _____

4. **A musical** Example: _____

    Definition: _____

5. **An opera** Example: _____

    Definition: _____

6. **A ballet** Example: _____

    Definition: _____

7. **A drama** Example: _____

    Definition: _____

8. **A comedy** Example: _____

    Definition: _____

9. **A tragedy** Example: _____

    Definition: _____

10. **A mystery play, book, or television series** Example: _____

    Definition: _____

11. **A documentary** Example: _____

    Definition: _____

12. **A concert** Example: _____

    Definition: _____

13. **A cultural event** Example: _____

    Definition: _____

14. **A sporting event** Example: _____

    Definition: _____

My Favorite Television Program Is

_____.

Topics: Television, entertainment, writing and
delivering a report

*Pick one of your favorite television programs to watch at home. Then
complete the information and report on the program to the class.*

Name of series or program: _____

Name of episode: _____

Day/Date: _____

Time: from _____ to _____ A.M. _____ P.M. _____

Station/Channel: _____

Type of program? News _____   Situation comedy _____

Educational _____   Soap opera _____

Film/movie _____   Sporting event _____

Drama _____   Other _____

Main characters: _____

_____

Plot or story line (you may use notes): _____

_____

_____

_____

_____

What did you like or dislike about this program?

_____

_____

_____

Would you recommend this program to your classmates? Why or why
not?

_____

_____

Marriage Customs

Topic: Marriage customs in different cultures

In small groups, discuss marriage customs. Have one person take notes and report your discussion to the class.

1. How do a man and a woman get engaged in your home country? Do the families of the bride and groom arrange the marriage? Does the man ask the woman? Do the couple need permission from their parents? At what age do people usually get married?

   _____

   _____

   _____

2. Is the wedding ceremony civil or religious? Do the bride and groom exchange rings? How long does the wedding ceremony last? Where does it usually take place? Are other people invited to the wedding ceremony? Who? Are there any special customs?

   _____

   _____

   _____

3. Is there a reception after the ceremony? What do people do at the reception? Do people give the newlywed couple wedding presents? What kind of presents? What special food is served?

   _____

   _____

   _____

4. Do newlyweds go on a honeymoon after the wedding and reception? Where do they go? What do they do?

   _____

   _____

   _____

5. How long do marriages last in your home country? What happens if the married couple no longer want to be married? Can married couples divorce? How?

   _____

   _____

   _____

Marriage Customs (continued)

Topics: Marriage customs, writing a paragraph of comparison/contrast

Write a paragraph comparing and contrasting the way weddings are arranged and celebrated in the United States and in your home country.

Use some of these words and phrases.

like	different than	more. . . than
the same as	in contrast with	— er than
both	compared to	while
but		unlike

_____

_____

_____

_____

_____

_____

_____

_____

After you finish your paragraph, have your teacher look it over, correct it, and comment on it. Then rewrite it with the necessary corrections.

_____

_____

_____

_____

_____

_____

_____

Public Health Facilities

Topics: Using telephone directories, making calls of inquiry

Look up the telephone number for these health facilities. Then call to make sure you have the right facility, the location, the hours open for service, and the services available.

1. Medicare   Telephone: _____ Days, hours <u>M, W, 9–1 P.M.</u>
   Location _____
   Services available _____
   _____

2. Regional Poison Center
   Telephone: _____ Days, hours _____
   Location _____
   Services available _____
   _____

3. Planned Parenthood   Telephone: _____ Days, hours _____
   Location _____
   Services available _____
   _____

4. Where to get a child a physical or immunizations for school.
   Facility _____
   Telephone: _____ Days, hours _____
   Location _____
   Services available _____
   _____

5. Where to go if you have a medical emergency.
   _____

   Telephone: _____ Days, hours _____
   Location _____
   Services available _____
   _____

Entertainment Events

With the class or in a small group, decide on an entertainment event, a museum, or other place of interest for the group to visit. Find out how to reach the place by public transportation. After attending the event or visiting the place of interest, answer the questions.

Event or place of interest: _____

What: _____

Where: _____

When: _____

Cost (if any): _____

General description: _____

_____

_____

_____

How did you get there? _____

What did you like the most and the least about the event or place?

_____

_____

_____

_____

Would you recommend this entertainment event or place of interest to your fellow classmates? Why/why not?

_____

_____

_____

_____

_____

✓ Summary: Recreation and Leisure Activities Checklist

Check (✓) one.

Yes   No   Need more practice

☐ ☐ ☐ I can talk about and describe recreational activities. (example: p. 22)

☐ ☐ ☐ I can use information collected to write a paragraph. (example: p. 23)

☐ ☐ ☐ I can write and present a three- to five-minute presentation. (example: p. 24)

☐ ☐ ☐ I can talk about and discuss various entertainment events. (example: p. 26)

☐ ☐ ☐ I can talk about and describe my favorite television program. (example: p. 28)

☐ ☐ ☐ I can talk about marriage customs in the United States and compare and contrast with my home country's. (example: p. 29–30)

☐ ☐ ☐ I can talk about public health facilities and services (example p. 31)

Write two other things you can say or do in English.

I can _____ .

I can _____ .

_____
Signature

Teacher's comments: _____

_____

Unit 3 On Writing

TOPICS

▲ Thesaurus
▲ Essay organization
▲ Report writing
▲ Appropriate or acceptable behavior
▲ A short book or story report

LANGUAGE FUNCTIONS

On completion, students will have used English for:

▲ factual information: to analyze, to evaluate, to paraphrase, to summarize.
▲ social and interpersonal relations: to express values, to express judgment.

LANGUAGE FORMS

On completion, students will have used the following structures:

▲ **Sentence types**
  Complex sentences

LANGUAGE SKILLS

Listening: On completion, students will have:

▲ demonstrated understanding of conversation in encounters with native speakers with little repetition or rewording.
▲ demonstrated understanding of descriptions and narrations of factual and technical material.

Speaking: On completion, students will have:

▲ spoken fluently in most formal and informal conversations on practical and social topics, except when under tension or pressure.
▲ spoken with some fluency on technical subjects or on special fields of interest related to academic pursuits or work demands.
▲ demonstrated control of grammatical patterns.

Reading: On completion, students will have:

▲ read authentic printed material and prose on familiar topics.
▲ read short stories and other recreational literature.
▲ interpreted main ideas and key points in technical material in their own fields of interest.
▲ applied appropriate reading strategies for understanding content on unfamiliar topics or in technical information.
▲ used syntactic clues to interpret the meaning of complex sentences and new vocabulary.
▲ reacted personally to reading materials by making judgments or prioritizing values.

Writing: On completion, students will have:

▲ punctuated paragraphs, making only minor errors.
▲ written paragraphs on familiar topics, using the techniques of comparison/contrast, cause/effect, generalization/example, and exposition.
▲ taken notes and written simple outlines of reading passages and lectures.

Writing Uppercase Cursive Letters

Topic: Uppercase cursive letters A – M

Trace and copy the letters.

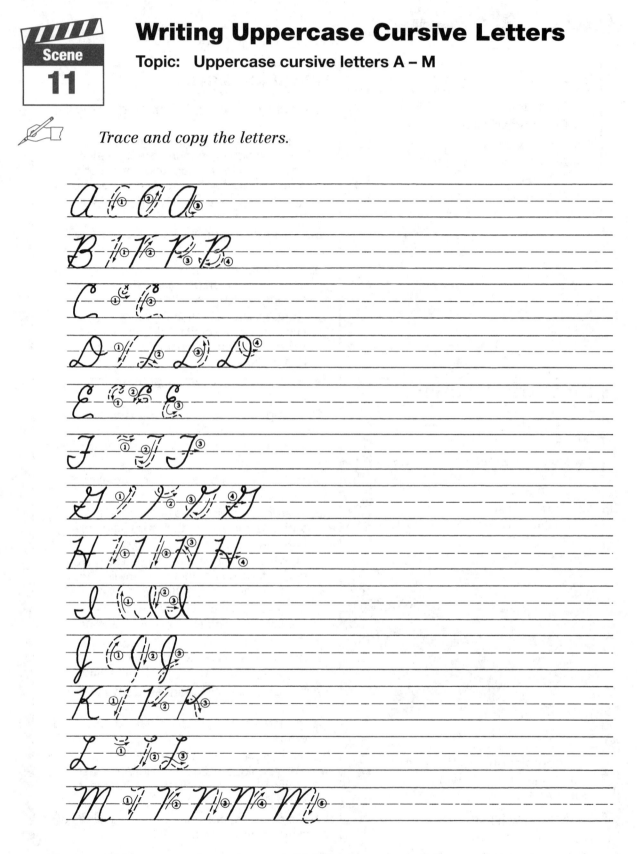

Writing Uppercase Cursive Letters
(continued)

Topic: Uppercase cursive letters N – Z

Trace and copy the letters.

Scene 12

Writing Lowercase Cursive Letters

Topic: Lowercase cursive letters a – m

Trace and copy the letters.

Writing Lowercase Cursive Letters
(continued)

Scene 12

Topic: Lowercase cursive letters n – z

Trace and copy the letters.

Practice
12

Writing Cursive Letter Combinations

Topic: Combining two or more cursive letters

Look at the letter combinations. Write them in cursive

ae

ao

be

ba

bo

by

co

mn

yr

op

on

stop

open

Practice 12

Writing Cursive Letter Combinations
(continued)

Topic: Combining three or more cursive letters as words

Look at the words. Write them in cursive.

got

for

how

come

have

when

with

talk

right

large

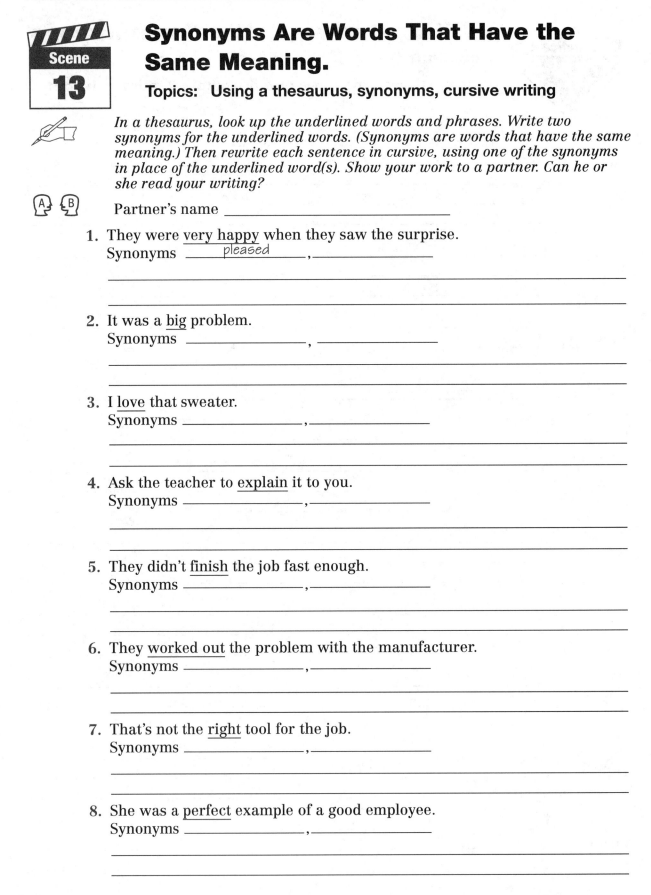

Scene 13

Synonyms Are Words That Have the Same Meaning.

Topics: Using a thesaurus, synonyms, cursive writing

In a thesaurus, look up the underlined words and phrases. Write two synonyms for the underlined words. (Synonyms are words that have the same meaning.) Then rewrite each sentence in cursive, using one of the synonyms in place of the underlined word(s). Show your work to a partner. Can he or she read your writing?

Partner's name _____

1. They were <u>very happy</u> when they saw the surprise.
   Synonyms ____pleased____ , _____

   _____

   _____

2. It was a <u>big</u> problem.
   Synonyms _____ , _____

   _____

   _____

3. I <u>love</u> that sweater.
   Synonyms _____ , _____

   _____

   _____

4. Ask the teacher to <u>explain</u> it to you.
   Synonyms _____ , _____

   _____

   _____

5. They didn't <u>finish</u> the job fast enough.
   Synonyms _____ , _____

   _____

   _____

6. They <u>worked out</u> the problem with the manufacturer.
   Synonyms _____ , _____

   _____

   _____

7. That's not the <u>right</u> tool for the job.
   Synonyms _____ , _____

   _____

   _____

8. She was a <u>perfect</u> example of a good employee.
   Synonyms _____ , _____

   _____

   _____

Clueword

Topic: Synonyms

Have fun playing this game in a group of four, with two people on each team.

Each player writes five words on a piece of paper and exchanges his or her list with a member of the opposite team. The team members do not show their new lists to each other. Player A1 looks at the first word on his or her list and says a synonym for the word. Player A2, his team member, tries to guess the mystery word. If he guesses correctly, Team A gets 5 points. If the guess is incorrect, Player A1 gives another synonym for the mystery word, Player A2 guesses again and, if the guess is correct, earns 4 points. Each team has five tries to guess each mystery word, earning one point less for each try needed. (The fifth try earns only 1 point.)

Next, Team B plays, with Player B1 supplying the synonyms and Player B2 trying to guess the first mystery word. Third, Player A2 supplies synonyms for the second word on his new list, and Player A1 tries to guess it. The game continues until both teams have used up all five of their mystery words, with the team members taking turns giving the clues. The team with the most points wins the game.

Examples of synonyms:

     for *happy*: glad, cheerful, merry, delighted, jolly, overjoyed

     for *market*: store, bazaar, emporium, mall, mart, shop, grocery

     for *fall* (verb): drop, plunge, plummet, descend, go down, go lower

     for *railroad car*: Pullman, sleeping car, caboose, baggage car, freight
                    car, flatcar, sleeper

     for *slow* (adj): idle, lazy, tardy, postponing, dragging

     for *large*: big, vast, huge, enormous, gigantic, immense, gross

Write some synonyms of your choice.

Word	Synonyms
_____	_____
_____	_____
_____	_____
_____	_____
_____	_____

Essay Questions Require Much More Thought than a Simple Answer.

Topics: Organizing an essay, written exams

Students at all grade levels in the United States are asked essay questions on school exams. Answering these types of questions requires much more thought and information than a simple answer and allows the students to show their depth of understanding of the subject. A typical essay response includes several components.

1. An introduction which, includes statement of topic paragraph

2. Supporting paragraphs, which
- illustrate
- explain
- describe
- argue

3. A conclusion, which refers back to the topic sentence and concludes the writer's thoughts

You have twenty minutes to answer one of the essay questions below. First write an outline on this page to summarize what you will include in the essay. Then write out your essay on the next page. Your essay should be three to five paragraphs long.

Topic 1. Is it important to speak English to be successful in the United States? Why or why not?

Topic 2. Is it easier to find work in the United States than in your home country? Why or why not?

Outline

_____

_____

_____

_____

_____

_____

_____

_____

Practice 14

Writing an Essay

Topics: Organizing and writing an essay from an outline

After completing your outline, use this space to write your essay. You may want to use cursive script.

_____

_____

_____

_____

_____

_____

_____

_____

_____

_____

_____

_____

_____

_____

_____

_____

_____

_____

_____

_____

_____

_____

Name _____   **Date** _____

Research and Read About Your Topic.

Topics: Report and term paper writing

Researching and Writing a Report or Term Paper

1. Plan your time in advance. If you have a time limit, divide the work into parts so that you can set up a schedule in which to complete the work.

2. Define a *general* topic. This should not be too limiting because you are going to narrow down your topic after you do some research.

3. Survey several sources to get an idea of the scope of your topic. These sources can be resource texts, journals, other books, or even magazines.

4. Make a bibliography card for each source you use. These sources will make up your bibliography. Include
   - Title
   - Author
   - Publisher and date of publication
   - Units, chapters, and pages referenced

5. Decide on a general outline form to use. Begin your outline.

6. Research and read more about your topic. On index cards write notes, exact quotes, paraphrases, and/or summaries of the information you find. Remember to include the title and page reference of the source on each card. You will not need to include the complete publishing information because that already appears on your bibliography cards.

7. Now that you have a lot of information, you can limit your topic. Revise your outline into a logical presentation of your new limited topic.

8. Write the first rough draft. Then do additional research or reading to complete or add to the information or ideas you plan to include.

9. Revise and rewrite your rough draft.
   - Insert any division headings you want to use.
   - Vary the length of your sentences to make them more interesting.
   - Try to use a variety of connectors:

to add more information:	to compare:	to contrast:	to explain:
and also in addition besides	like same as	but different than the same as	for example, for instance, in fact, because

10. In your conclusion, include a reference to your topic sentence, perhaps using *as stated, I believe, therefore,* or *in conclusion.*

11. Reread your paper to make sure it is clear and logical.

12. Use your bibliography cards to prepare your bibliography. Several forms are possible; each field has its own standard.

13. Prepare a final draft on a typewriter, word processor, or computer.

Practice 15

Writing a Report
Topics: Report or term paper writing

Write a two-page report on one of these topics. Use at least two sources. They can be books, reference texts, encyclopedias, journals, magazines, or newspapers. Prepare your rough draft. Then use the space provided to write your final copy. Remember to include a bibliography.

Civil Rights	Intercultural Communication
U.S. Politics	Language Learning
Entertainment	Your own topic

_____

_____

_____

_____

_____

_____

_____

_____

_____

_____

_____

_____

_____

_____

_____

_____

_____

_____

_____

_____

_____

_____

_____

_____

Writing a Report (continued)

Topics: Report or term paper writing

_____

_____

_____

_____

_____

_____

_____

_____

_____

_____

_____

_____

_____

_____

_____

_____

_____

_____

_____

_____

_____

_____

_____

_____

_____

_____

_____

_____

What Does It Mean?

Cross-Cultural Discussion 3

First, read each situation and write what you think it means. Then discuss your answers in a small group. Have one person take notes and report your discussion to the entire class. Is the behavior acceptable? If not, why not?

1. A young man winks at a lady he doesn't know.

   In the United States, _____

   In your home country, _____

2. Two people greet each other by kissing on the mouth.

   In the United States, _____

   In your home country, _____

3. A person speaking to you stands so close that he or she is touching you.

   In the United States, _____

   In your home country, _____

4. A young man whistles at a passing girl.

   In the United States, _____

   In your home country, _____

5. Two people are walking down the street, holding hands.

   In the United States, _____

   In your home country, _____

6. The person speaking to you won't look you in the eye.

   In the United States, _____

   In your home country, _____

Supplemental Activity 3

Writing a Short Book Report

Ask your teacher to recommend, or use the library to find, a book or short story to read. Read it. Then use the form to write a short book or story report.

Some titles you might consider:
   The Old Man and the Sea by Ernest Hemingway
   A collection of modern short stories, such as James Thurber's
   A Christmas Carol by Charles Dickens
   I Know Why the Caged Bird Sings by Maya Angelou

1. Title: _____

2. Author: _____

3. Main characters: _____

   _____

4. Setting: Where and when the story takes place

   _____

   _____

5. Plot or storyline _____

   _____

   _____

   _____

   _____

   _____

6. Author's intent: Why do you think the author wrote this piece?

   _____

   _____

7. Your opinion: What did you like or not like about the story? Would you recommend this story to a friend?

   _____

   _____

   _____

On Writing Checklist

Check (✓) one.

Yes   **No**   **Need more practice**

☐ ☐ ☐ I can write and read cursive writing.
(example: p. 41)

☐ ☐ ☐ I can use a thesaurus to find synonyms of
words and phrases.
(example: p. 42)

☐ ☐ ☐ I can organize and write a short essay.
(example: p. 45)

☐ ☐ ☐ I can organize and write a short report.
(example: p. 47)

☐ ☐ ☐ I can talk about appropriateness of certain
actions, such as winking, whistling, touching.
(example: p. 49)

☐ ☐ ☐ I can write a short book report.
(example: p. 50)

Write two other things you can say or do in English.

I can _____ .

I can _____ .

_____
Signature

Teacher's comments: _____

_____

Unit 4 Democratic Government

TOPICS

▲ U.S. politics
▲ The U.S. government
▲ The Bill of Rights
▲ Personal legal rights
▲ Tax forms
▲ Crime and punishment
▲ Visiting a court house

LANGUAGE FUNCTIONS

On completion, students will have used English for:

▲ factual information: to analyze, to evaluate, to paraphrase, to summarize.
▲ social and interpersonal relations: to express values, to express judgment.

LANGUAGE FORMS

On completion, students will have used the following structures:

▲ **Sentence types**

Noun clauses ("What the weatherperson predicts is not always correct.")

LANGUAGE SKILLS

Listening: On completion, students will have:

▲ demonstrated understanding of descriptions and narrations of factual and technical material.

Speaking: On completion, students will have:

▲ spoken fluently in most formal and informal conversations on practical and social topics, except when under tension or pressure.
▲ demonstrated control of grammatical patterns—including perfect tenses, passive constructions, complex sentences, and the conditional tense—although with some hesitation when choosing accurate grammar and appropriate vocabulary.

Reading: On completion, students will have:

▲ read authentic printed material and prose on familiar topics.
▲ interpreted main ideas and key points from technical material in their own fields of interest.
▲ applied appropriate reading strategies for understanding content on unfamiliar topics or in technical information.
▲ used syntactic clues to interpret the meaning of complex sentences and new vocabulary.
▲ analyzed an author's point of view by making inferences.
▲ reacted to reading materials by making personal judgments or by prioritizing values.

Writing: On completion, students will have:

▲ punctuated paragraphs, making only minor errors.
▲ written paragraphs on familiar topics.
▲ taken notes from lectures.
▲ written simple outlines of reading passages and lectures.
▲ written summaries of reading passages.

The U.S. Government Has Three Branches.

Topic: Tripartite government

Listen to the lecture.

The United States has three branches of government.

   I.   **The legislative branch** of the government (Congress) proposes and makes laws. Congress is made up of the Senate and the House of Representatives. There are 100 senators, or two senators from each state. Senators are elected for six-year terms. The House of Representatives is made up of 435 congressmen and congresswomen who are elected every two years. The number of congressmen and congresswomen varies from state to state and is based on the state's population.

   II.   **The executive branch** of the government signs laws into effect and enforces laws. The president, vice-president, and cabinet are members of the executive branch of the government. The president and vice-president are elected in a national election that takes place every four years in November. A president may serve only two terms.

   III.   **The judicial branch** of the government explains and interprets the laws. The Supreme Court and federal courts make up the judicial branch of the government. The Supreme Court is the highest court in the United States. Supreme Court justices are appointed by the president and approved by the Senate. The nine Supreme Court justices are appointed for life.

Listen again and answer the questions.

1. Name the three branches of the U.S. government.

   a. _____   b. _____   c. _____

2. A senator proposes and _____.

3. The president and vice-president serve for _____.

4. The _____ Supreme Court justices _____

_____.

5. Are all members of the U.S. government elected?

_____.

The Executive and Legislative Branches

Topics: U.S. government officials and elected representatives

Answer the questions. If you don't know an answer, look it up in the library in an encyclopedia, or in a recent telephone directory. Then compare your answers with a partner's.

Partner's name _____

1. The president of the United States is _____.

2. The vice-president of the United States is _____.

3. The two U.S. senators for my state are _____
   and _____.

4. The congressman or congresswoman for my district is

   _____.

5. The president or leader of my home country is _____

   _____.

6. Why are there 100 senators? _____

   _____.

7. Why are there more members in the House of Representatives than
   in the Senate? Is this fair? _____

   _____

   _____.

8. Why do you think Supreme Court justices are appointed for life?

   _____

   _____.

9. Do you think it is a good idea to have three separate branches of
   government? Why or why not? _____

   _____.

Write a short paragraph comparing or contrasting your home country's national government and the U.S. system of government.

_____

_____

_____

_____

The Bill of Rights

Scene 17

Topics: Personal rights, the U.S. Constitution

The U.S. Constitution, which set up the three branches of the federal government, did not mention citizens' rights. Changes to the original Constitution are called amendments. The first ten amendments to the Constitution are called the Bill of Rights, and all guaranty citizens' rights.

Amendments to the U.S. Constitution

1st: the freedom of speech, of religion, and of the press; the freedom to assemble (to meet in groups); the freedom to petition the government (to ask it to change things)

2nd: the right of the people to keep and bear arms

3rd: the guaranty that no homeowner be required to give lodgings to a soldier without the homeowner's consent

4th: protects citizens from unreasonable searches of their persons or their homes

5th: protects people from being tried twice for the same crime
from having to testify against themselves in court
from having their life, liberty, or property taken away
without due process of law

6th: grants persons the right to a speedy and public trial by jury
the right to know what he or she is accused of
the right to face his or her accusers
the right to be represented in a trial by a lawyer

7th: guarantees the right of trial by jury and prohibits reexamining any tried case

8th: prohibits excessive bail and fines and cruel and unusual punishment

9th: protects unenumerated (not named) residual rights of the people

10th: guarantees to the people and the states the powers not delegated by the Constitution to the federal government.

Talk about the different amendments above with the class. Then complete the sentences.

1. Amendment _____ guarantees freedom from cruel and unusual punishment.

2. Amendment _____ guarantees freedom of speech.

3. Amendment _____ guarantees the right to a speedy trial.

4. Amendment _____ guarantees freedom of religion.

5. Amendment _____ guarantees the right to bear arms.

6. Amendment _____ guarantees the right to privacy.

The Miranda Rule

Topic: Personal legal rights

The Miranda Rule is a Supreme Court decision that states these points. If you are arrested, the law enforcement officer arresting you will inform you of your rights. You will be warned:

1. that you have the right to remain silent.
2. that anything you say may be used as evidence against you.
3. that you have the right to be represented by an attorney.
4. that if you can't afford an attorney, one will be appointed for you before you are questioned, if you desire.

Read the description of the Miranda Rule. Then answer the questions in complete sentences.

1. You are put under arrest by a police officer. Do you have to answer any questions about what you were just doing? Why?

    _____

    _____

    _____

2. You are put under arrest by a police officer. You want to talk to an attorney before you answer any questions, but you don't have any money to pay for one. What would you do or say? Why?

    _____

    _____

    _____

3. You are put under arrest, and the police officer asks you if you just robbed a store. You didn't. What would you do or say? Why?

    _____

    _____

Discuss your responses with a small group or the entire class.

Politics and Political Parties

 Look at the political campaign materials above. Then answer the questions and share your answers with the class.

1. Name two political parties in the United States.

   _____   _____

2. Do you have different political parties in your home country? Describe and explain your answer.

   _____

   _____

   _____

3. Are political leaders elected in your home country? How often? If NO, how are they chosen or appointed?

   _____

   _____

   _____

4. Do you think political elections for national leaders are the best way to choose or appoint national leaders? Write a paragraph explaining why or why not.

   _____

   _____

   _____

   _____

Form 1040

Department of the Treasury—Internal Revenue Service

U.S. Individual Income Tax Return (P) 1995

IRS Use Only—Do not write or staple in this space.

For the year Jan. 1–Dec. 31, 1995, or other tax year beginning _____ , 1995, ending _____ , 19 ___ OMB No. 1545-0074

Label
(See instructions on page 11.)

Use the IRS label. Otherwise, please print or type.

L A B E L   H E R E

Your first name and initial | Last name

Your social security number

If a joint return, spouse's first name and initial | Last name

Spouse's social security number

Home address (number and street). If you have a P.O. box, see page 11. | Apt. no.

City, town or post office, state, and ZIP code. If you have a foreign address, see page 11.

For Privacy Act and Paperwork Reduction Act Notice, see page 7.

Presidential Election Campaign
(See page 11.)

▶ Do you want $3 to go to this fund? . . . .

If a joint return, does your spouse want $3 to go to this fund? . . . .

Yes | No

Note: Checking "Yes" will not change your tax or reduce your refund.

Filing Status
(See page 11.)

Check only one box.

1 ☐ Single

2 ☐ Married filing joint return (even if only one had income)

3 ☐ Married filing separate return. Enter spouse's social security no. above and full name here. ▶

4 ☐ Head of household (with qualifying person). (See page 12.) If the qualifying person is a child but not your dependent, enter this child's name here. ▶

5 ☐ Qualifying widow(er) with dependent child (year spouse died ▶ 19 ___). (See page 12.)

Exemptions
(See page 12.)

6a ☐ **Yourself.** If your parent (or someone else) can claim you as a dependent on his or her tax return, **do not** check box 6a. But be sure to check the box on line 33b on page 2

b ☐ **Spouse** . . . .

No. of boxes checked on 6a and 6b

No. of your children on 6c who:
● lived with you
● didn't live with you due to divorce or separation (see page 14)

Dependents on 6c not entered above

c **Dependents:**

(1) First name Last name	(2) Dependent's social security number. If born in 1995, see page 13.	(3) Dependent's relationship to you	(4) No. of months lived in your home in 1995

If more than six dependents, see page 13.

d If your child didn't live with you but is claimed as your dependent under a pre-1985 agreement, check here ▶ ☐

e Total number of exemptions claimed . . . .

Add numbers entered on lines above ▶

Income

Attach Copy B of your Forms W-2, W-2G, and 1099-R here.

If you did not get a W-2, see page 14.

Enclose, but do not attach, your payment and payment voucher. See page 33.

7 Wages, salaries, tips, etc. Attach Form(s) W-2 . . . . | 7 |

8a **Taxable** interest income (see page 15). Attach Schedule B if over $400 . . . . | 8a |

b Tax-exempt interest (see page 15). DON'T include on line 8a | 8b |

9 Dividend income. Attach Schedule B if over $400 . . . . | 9 |

10 Taxable refunds, credits, or offsets of state and local income taxes (see page 15) . . | 10 |

11 Alimony received . . . . | 11 |

12 Business income or (loss). Attach Schedule C or C-EZ . . . . | 12 |

13 Capital gain or (loss). If required, attach Schedule D (see page 16) . . . . | 13 |

14 Other gains or (losses). Attach Form 4797 . . . . | 14 |

15a Total IRA distributions . | 15a | b Taxable amount (see page 16) | 15b |

16a Total pensions and annuities | 16a | b Taxable amount (see page 16) | 16b |

17 Rental real estate, royalties, partnerships, S corporations, trusts, etc. Attach Schedule E | 17 |

18 Farm income or (loss). Attach Schedule F . . . . | 18 |

19 Unemployment compensation (see page 17) . . . . | 19 |

20a Social security benefits | 20a | b Taxable amount (see page 18) | 20b |

21 Other income. List type and amount—see page 18 _____ | 21 |

22 Add the amounts in the far right column for lines 7 through 21. This is your **total income** ▶ | 22 |

Adjustments to Income

23a Your IRA deduction (see page 19) . . . . | 23a |

b Spouse's IRA deduction (see page 19) . . . | 23b |

24 Moving expenses. Attach Form 3903 or 3903-F . | 24 |

25 One-half of self-employment tax . . . . | 25 |

26 Self-employed health insurance deduction (see page 21) | 26 |

27 Keogh & self-employed SEP plans. If SEP, check ▶ ☐ | 27 |

28 Penalty on early withdrawal of savings . . . | 28 |

29 Alimony paid. Recipient's SSN ▶ _____ | 29 |

30 Add lines 23a through 29. These are your **total adjustments** . . . . . . ▶ | 30 |

Adjusted Gross Income

31 Subtract line 30 from line 22. This is your **adjusted gross income.** If less than $26,673 and a child lived with you (less than $9,230 if a child didn't live with you), see "Earned Income Credit" on page 27 ▶ | 31 |

Cat. No. 12599G

Form **1040** (1995)

Form 1040 (1995)   Page **2**

Tax Compu-tation (See page 23.)	32	Amount from line 31 (adjusted gross income)	32
	33a	Check if: ☐ **You** were 65 or older, ☐ Blind; ☐ **Spouse** was 65 or older, ☐ Blind. Add the number of boxes checked above and enter the total here ▶ 33a	
	b	If your parent (or someone else) can claim you as a dependent, check here ▶ 33b ☐	
	c	If you are married filing separately and your spouse itemizes deductions or you are a dual-status alien, see page 23 and check here ▶ 33c ☐	
	34	Enter the larger of your: { **Itemized deductions** from Schedule A, line 28, **OR** **Standard deduction** shown below for your filing status. **But if you checked any box on line 33a or b**, go to page 23 to find your standard deduction. If you checked **box 33c**, your standard deduction is zero. • Single—$3,900 • Married filing jointly or Qualifying widow(er)—$6,550 • Head of household—$5,750 • Married filing separately—$3,275 }	34
	35	Subtract line 34 from line 32	35
If you want the IRS to figure your tax, see page 35.	36	If line 32 is $86,025 or less, multiply $2,500 by the total number of exemptions claimed on line 6e. If line 32 is over $86,025, see the worksheet on page 23 for the amount to enter	36
	37	**Taxable income.** Subtract line 36 from line 35. If line 36 is more than line 35, enter -0-	37
	38	Tax. Check if from a ☐ Tax Table, b ☐ Tax Rate Schedules, c ☐ Capital Gain Tax Worksheet, or d ☐ Form 8615 (see page 24). Amount from Form(s) 8814 ▶ e _____	38
	39	Additional taxes. Check if from a ☐ Form 4970 b ☐ Form 4972	39
	40	Add lines 38 and 39 ▶	40

Credits (See page 24.)	41	Credit for child and dependent care expenses. Attach Form 2441	41	
	42	Credit for the elderly or the disabled. Attach Schedule R	42	
	43	Foreign tax credit. Attach Form 1116	43	
	44	Other credits (see page 25). Check if from a ☐ Form 3800 b ☐ Form 8396 c ☐ Form 8801 d ☐ Form (specify) _____	44	
	45	Add lines 41 through 44		45
	46	Subtract line 45 from line 40. If line 45 is more than line 40, enter -0- ▶		46

Other Taxes (See page 25.)	47	Self-employment tax. Attach Schedule SE	47
	48	Alternative minimum tax. Attach Form 6251	48
	49	Recapture taxes. Check if from a ☐ Form 4255 b ☐ Form 8611 c ☐ Form 8828	49
	50	Social security and Medicare tax on tip income not reported to employer. Attach Form 4137	50
	51	Tax on qualified retirement plans, including IRAs. If required, attach Form 5329	51
	52	Advance earned income credit payments from Form W-2	52
	53	Household employment taxes. Attach Schedule H	53
	54	Add lines 46 through 53. This is your **total tax** ▶	54

Payments Attach Forms W-2, W-2G, and 1099-R on the front.	55	Federal income tax withheld. If any is from Form(s) 1099, check ▶ ☐	55	
	56	1995 estimated tax payments and amount applied from 1994 return	56	
	57	**Earned income credit.** Attach Schedule EIC if you have a qualifying child. Nontaxable earned income: amount ▶ _____ and type ▶	57	
	58	Amount paid with Form 4868 (extension request)	58	
	59	Excess social security and RRTA tax withheld (see page 32)	59	
	60	Other payments. Check if from a ☐ Form 2439 b ☐ Form 4136	60	
	61	Add lines 55 through 60. These are your **total payments** ▶		61

Refund or Amount You Owe	62	If line 61 is more than line 54, subtract line 54 from line 61. This is the amount you **OVERPAID**	62
	63	Amount of line 62 you want **REFUNDED TO YOU** ▶	63
	64	Amount of line 62 you want **APPLIED TO YOUR 1996 ESTIMATED TAX** ▶ 64	
	65	If line 54 is more than line 61, subtract line 61 from line 54. This is the **AMOUNT YOU OWE.** For details on how to pay and use **Form 1040-V**, Payment Voucher, see page 33 ▶	65
	66	Estimated tax penalty (see page 33). Also include on line 65 66	

Sign Here Keep a copy of this return for your records.	Under penalties of perjury, I declare that I have examined this return and accompanying schedules and statements, and to the best of my knowledge and belief, they are true, correct, and complete. Declaration of preparer (other than taxpayer) is based on all information of which preparer has any knowledge.	
	Your signature	Date Your occupation
	Spouse's signature. If a joint return, BOTH must sign.	Date Spouse's occupation

Paid Preparer's Use Only	Preparer's signature	Date Check if self-employed ☐ Preparer's social security no.
	Firm's name (or yours if self-employed) and address	EIN ZIP code

♻ *Printed on recycled paper*   ☆ U.S. Government Printing Office: 1995 - 389 - 540

April 15th—Taxes Due!

Scene 19

Topics: 1040 tax form, tax vocabulary

April 15 is an important date for all U.S. taxpayers. That is the date that their federal and state income taxes are due.

Work in a small group to match the tax words with their meaning. If you cannot figure out the meaning of a word, look it up in a dictionary or other resource book.

1. ___ IRS
2. ___ tax return
3. ___ spouse
4. ___ joint return
5. ___ filing status
6. ___ W-2
7. ___ witholdings
8. ___ 1040, 1040EZ
9. ___ exemptions
10. ___ dependents
11. ___ gross income
12. ___ interest
13. ___ adjustments
14. ___ tax table
15. ___ refund

a. individual tax forms
b. table used to figure taxes owed
c. Internal Revenue Service
d. how you file: single or married
e. deductions and credits
f. husband (or wife) and children
g. taxes withheld by employer
h. one tax form filed by two people
i. money returned to you by the IRS
j. wage and tax statement from employer
k. money earned on savings
l. due on April 15 of every year
m. total money you earned before anything was taken out
n. income not subject to taxation
o. husband or wife

Look at Juan Garcia's W-2 for 1995 and answer the questions.

Form W-2 Wage and Tax Statement 1995

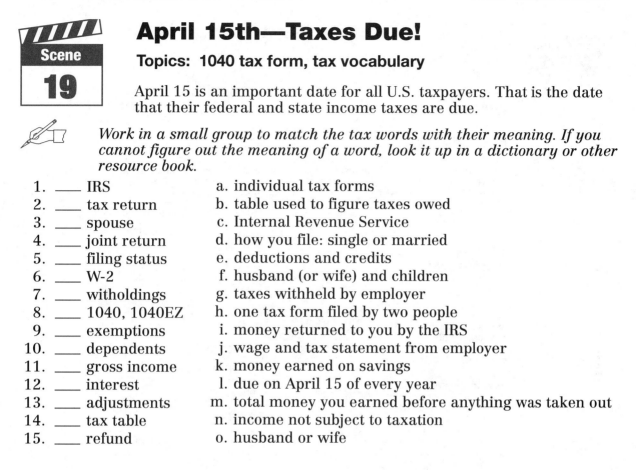

Copy 1 To Be Filed with Employee's Federal Tax Return		1. Gross Wages, tips, other compensation $28,950	
Employer's name, address, and Zip code **Acme Manufacturing**	Employee's social security number 111-22-3333	2. Federal income tax paid $5,280	
	3. Social Security tax withheld $1,790	4. Medicare tax withheld $420.00	
Employee's name, address, and Zip code Juan Garcia 124 5th Street Los Angeles, CA 92801		6. Other	
	7. State income tax withheld		

1. How much is Juan's gross income? $ _____

2. How much did Juan pay in federal income tax? $_____

3. How much did he pay for Social Security? $ _____

4. Do you get a W-2 from your employer? _____

Name _____   **Date** _____

Determining Who Should File

Topics: Taxes, reading a chart

Look over the chart, whose rules apply to all U.S. citizens and resident aliens. Then answer the questions and check your answers with a partner.

Partner's name _____

To use this chart, first find your marital status at the end of 1995. Then, read across to find your filing status and age at the end of 1995. You must file a return if your **gross income**** was at least the amount shown in the last column.

Marital status	Filing status	Age*	Gross income**
Single (including divorced and legally separated)	Single	under 65	$6,400
		65 or older	7,350
	Head of household (see page 12)	under 65	$8,250
		65 or older	9,200
Married with a child and living apart from your spouse during the last 6 months of 1995	Head of household (see page 12)	under 65	$8,250
		65 or older	9,200
Married and living with your spouse at end of 1995 (or on the date your spouse died)	Married, joint return	under 65 (both spouses)	$11,550
		65 or older (one spouse)	12,300
		65 or older (both spouses)	13,050
	Married, separate return	any age	$2,500
Married, not living with your spouse at end of 1995 (or on the date your spouse died)	Married, joint or separate return	any age	$2,500
Widowed before 1995 and not remarried in 1995	Single	under 65	$6,400
		65 or older	7,350
	Head of household	under 65	$8,250
		65 or older	9,200
	Qualifying widow(er) with dependent child (see page 12)	under 65	$9,050
		65 or older	9,800

* If you turned age 65 on January 1, 1996, you are considered to be age 65 at the end of 1995.

** **Gross income** means all income you received in the form of money, goods, property, and services that is not exempt from tax, including any gain on the sale of your home (even if you may exclude or postpone part or all of the gain). **Do not** include social security benefits unless you are married filing a separate return and you lived with your spouse at any time during 1995.

Use the chart to find out if these people should file a return.

Name	Filing Status	Age	Gross Income	Check yes	no
1. Pam Cho	Divorced	25 years old	$25,495	_____	_____
2. Misha Gorbin	Married filing jointly	30 years old	$31,500	_____	_____
3. Alex Rios	Widowed	67 years old	$ 6,500	_____	_____
4. You				_____	_____

**Lifeskills/
Workskills**

2

Completing a Tax Form for Juan Garcia

Topic: Completing a 1040 tax form

Use Juan Garcia's personal information on page 61 and this additional information on his W-2 to complete the first three parts of the tax form.

Name: Juan Garcia   Job: Mechanic

Filing status: Married filing jointly

Wife's name: Gloria Garcia   Job: Student

Wife's SS#: 555–44–3333   Other income: None

                                               Other exemptions: 0

Form **1040**	Department of the Treasury—Internal Revenue Service	**U.S. Individual Income Tax Return** (P) **1995**	IRS Use Only—Do not write or staple in this space.

Label
(See instructions on page 11.)

Use the IRS label. Otherwise, please print or type.

Presidential Election Campaign
(See page 11.)

For the year Jan. 1–Dec. 31, 1995, or other tax year beginning _____, 1995, ending _____, 19 ___   OMB No. 1545-0074

Your first name and initial | Last name | Your social security number

If a joint return, spouse's first name and initial | Last name | Spouse's social security number

Home address (number and street). If you have a P.O. box, see page 11. | Apt. no.

City, town or post office, state, and ZIP code. If you have a foreign address, see page 11.

For Privacy Act and Paperwork Reduction Act Notice, see page 7.

Do you want $3 to go to this fund? . . . .
If a joint return, does your spouse want $3 to go to this fund? . . . .

Yes | No | Note: Checking "Yes" will not change your tax or reduce your refund.

Filing Status
(See page 11.)

Check only one box.

1 ☐ Single
2 ☐ Married filing joint return (even if only one had income)
3 ☐ Married filing separate return. Enter spouse's social security no. above and full name here. ►
4 ☐ Head of household (with qualifying person). (See page 12.) If the qualifying person is a child but not your dependent, enter this child's name here. ►
5 ☐ Qualifying widow(er) with dependent child (year spouse died ► 19 ___). (See page 12.)

Exemptions
(See page 12.)

If more than six dependents, see page 13.

6a ☐ **Yourself.** If your parent (or someone else) can claim you as a dependent on his or her tax return, **do not** check box 6a. But be sure to check the box on line 33b on page 2

b ☐ **Spouse** . . . .

c **Dependents:**

(1) First name Last name	(2) Dependent's social security number. If born in 1995, see page 13.	(3) Dependent's relationship to you	(4) No. of months lived in your home in 1995

No. of boxes checked on 6a and 6b ___

No. of your children on 6c who:
• lived with you
• didn't live with you due to divorce or separation (see page 14)

Dependents on 6c not entered above

d If your child didn't live with you but is claimed as your dependent under a pre-1985 agreement, check here ► ☐
e Total number of exemptions claimed . . . .

Add numbers entered on lines above ►

Use the information and form above the answer the questions. Check your answers with a partner.

Partner's name _____

1. What year is this tax form for? _____

2. What is a joint return? _____

3. What would *you* personally check for your filing status? _____

   Why? _____

4. Does Juan have any exemptions other than himself? If "Yes," how many? ____

5. What did you fill in for Juan on line 6e?

   _____

Name _____   Date _____

Completing a Tax Form for Juan Garcia (continued)

Topic: Completing a 1040 tax form

Use Juan Garcia's information to complete the tax form.

Income				
Attach Copy B of your Forms W-2, W-2G, and 1099-R here.	7	Wages, salaries, tips, etc. Attach Form(s) W-2	7	
	8a	**Taxable** interest income (see page 15). Attach Schedule B if over $400	8a	
	b	**Tax-exempt** interest (see page 15). DON'T include on line 8a 8b		
If you did not get a W-2, see page 14.	9	Dividend income. Attach Schedule B if over $400	9	
	10	Taxable refunds, credits, or offsets of state and local income taxes (see page 15) . .	10	
	11	Alimony received	11	
	12	Business income or (loss). Attach Schedule C or C-EZ	12	
	13	Capital gain or (loss). If required, attach Schedule D (see page 16)	13	
Enclose, but do not attach, your payment and payment voucher. See page 33.	14	Other gains or (losses). Attach Form 4797	14	
	15a	Total IRA distributions . 15a	b Taxable amount (see page 16)	15b	
	16a	Total pensions and annuities 16a	b Taxable amount (see page 16)	16b	
	17	Rental real estate, royalties, partnerships, S corporations, trusts, etc. Attach Schedule E	17	
	18	Farm income or (loss). Attach Schedule F	18	
	19	Unemployment compensation (see page 17)	19	
	20a	Social security benefits 20a	b Taxable amount (see page 18)	20b	
	21	Other income. List type and amount—see page 18	21	
	22	Add the amounts in the far right column for lines 7 through 21. This is your **total income** ▶	22	
Adjustments to Income	23a	Your IRA deduction (see page 19)	23a	
	b	Spouse's IRA deduction (see page 19)	23b	
	24	Moving expenses. Attach Form 3903 or 3903-F	24	
	25	One-half of self-employment tax	25	
	26	Self-employed health insurance deduction (see page 21)	26	
	27	Keogh & self-employed SEP plans. If SEP, check ▶ ☐	27	
	28	Penalty on early withdrawal of savings	28	
	29	Alimony paid. Recipient's SSN ▶	29	
	30	Add lines 23a through 29. These are your **total adjustments** . . . . ▶	30	
Adjusted Gross Income	31	Subtract line 30 from line 22. This is your **adjusted gross income**. If less than $26,673 and a child lived with you (less than $9,230 if a child didn't live with you), see "Earned Income Credit" on page 27 ▶	31	

Cat. No. 12599G   Form **1040** (1995)

Answer the questions. Check your answers with a partner's.

Ⓐ Ⓑ   Partner's name _____

1. What did you enter on line 7?
   $ _____

2. What did you enter on line 11?
   $ _____

3. What was Juan's total income?
   $ _____

4. What were Juan's total adjustments?
   $ _____

5. What is Juan's Adjusted Gross Income?
   $ _____

Lifeskills/ Workskills

2

Completing a Tax Form for Juan Garcia (continued)

Topic: Completing a 1040 tax form

Use Juan Garcia's information to complete the tax form.

Form 1040 (1995)   Page **2**

Tax Compu-tation (See page 23.)	**32**	Amount from line 31 (adjusted gross income)	**32**
	33a	Check if: ☐ **You** were 65 or older, ☐ Blind; ☐ **Spouse** was 65 or older, ☐ Blind. Add the number of boxes checked above and enter the total here . . . . . ▶ **33a** ☐	
	b	If your parent (or someone else) can claim you as a dependent, check here . ▶ **33b** ☐	
	c	If you are married filing separately and your spouse itemizes deductions or you are a dual-status alien, see page 23 and check here. . . . . ▶ **33c** ☐	
	34	Enter the larger of your: { **Itemized deductions** from Schedule A, line 28, **OR** **Standard deduction** shown below for your filing status. **But if you checked any box on line 33a or b,** go to page 23 to find your standard deduction. If you checked **box 33c,** your standard deduction is zero. • Single—$3,900 • Married filing jointly or Qualifying widow(er)—$6,550 • Head of household—$5,750 • Married filing separately—$3,275 }	**34**
	35	Subtract line 34 from line 32	**35**
If you want the IRS to figure your tax, see page 35.	**36**	If line 32 is $86,025 or less, multiply $2,500 by the total number of exemptions claimed on line 6e. If line 32 is over $86,025, see the worksheet on page 23 for the amount to enter .	**36**
	37	**Taxable income.** Subtract line 36 from line 35. If line 36 is more than line 35, enter -0-	**37**
	38	Tax. Check if from a ☐ Tax Table, b ☐ Tax Rate Schedules, c ☐ Capital Gain Tax Work-sheet, or d ☐ Form 8615 (see page 24). Amount from Form(s) 8814 ▶ e _____	**38**
	39	Additional taxes. Check if from a ☐ Form 4970 b ☐ Form 4972	**39**
	40	Add lines 38 and 39. . . . . ▶	**40**

Answer the questions. Check your answers with a partner's.

Partner's name _____

1. What did you enter for Juan on line 32?

   $ _____

2. What did you enter for Juan on line 34?

   $ _____ Why? _____

   _____

3. What did you enter on line 35?

   $ _____

4. What did you enter on line 36?

   $ _____

Lifeskills/ Workskills

2

Completing a Tax Form for Juan Garcia (continued)

Topic: Completing a 1040 tax form

Use Juan Garcia's information to complete the tax form.

Credits	41	Credit for child and dependent care expenses. Attach Form 2441	41		
	42	Credit for the elderly or the disabled. Attach Schedule R . .	42		
(See page 24.)	43	Foreign tax credit. Attach Form 1116	43		
	44	Other credits (see page 25). Check if from **a** ☐ Form 3800 **b** ☐ Form 8396 **c** ☐ Form 8801 **d** ☐ Form (specify)_____	44		
	45	Add lines 41 through 44		45	
	46	Subtract line 45 from line 40. If line 45 is more than line 40, enter -0- . . . . . . ▶		46	
Other Taxes	47	Self-employment tax. Attach Schedule SE		47	
	48	Alternative minimum tax. Attach Form 6251		48	
(See page 25.)	49	Recapture taxes. Check if from **a** ☐ Form 4255 **b** ☐ Form 8611 **c** ☐ Form 8828 . .		49	
	50	Social security and Medicare tax on tip income not reported to employer. Attach Form 4137 .		50	
	51	Tax on qualified retirement plans, including IRAs. If required, attach Form 5329 . . .		51	
	52	Advance earned income credit payments from Form W-2		52	
	53	Household employment taxes. Attach Schedule H		53	
	54	Add lines 46 through 53. This is your **total tax** . . . . ▶		54	
Payments	55	Federal income tax withheld. If any is from Form(s) 1099, check ▶ ☐	55		
	56	1995 estimated tax payments and amount applied from 1994 return .	56		
Attach Forms W-2, W-2G, and 1099-R on the front.	57	**Earned income credit.** Attach Schedule EIC if you have a qualifying child. Nontaxable earned income: amount ▶ _____ and type ▶		57	
	58	Amount paid with Form 4868 (extension request)	58		
	59	Excess social security and RRTA tax withheld (see page 32)	59		
	60	Other payments. Check if from **a** ☐ Form 2439 **b** ☐ Form 4136	60		
	61	Add lines 55 through 60. These are your **total payments** . . . . ▶		61	

1. Check which forms you should attach to the front of your tax form.

   _____ a paycheck stub   _____ a W-2   _____ 1099-R

2. On which line would you enter a credit for the elderly or disabled?

   Line # _____

3. What do you enter on line 46 if line 40 is $750.00 and line 45 is $782.00?

   Amount $ _____

4. How do you figure out the total payments you've made?

   _____

   _____

Completing a Tax Form for Juan Garcia (continued)

Topic: Completing a 1040 tax form

Use Juan Garcia's information to complete the tax form.

Refund or Amount You Owe	62	If line 61 is more than line 54, subtract line 54 from line 61. This is the amount you OVERPAID.	62	
	63	Amount of line 62 you want **REFUNDED TO YOU**. ▶	63	
	64	Amount of line 62 you want **APPLIED TO YOUR 1996 ESTIMATED TAX** ▶ 64		
	65	If line 54 is more than line 61, subtract line 61 from line 54. This is the **AMOUNT YOU OWE**. For details on how to pay and use **Form 1040-V**, Payment Voucher, see page 33 . ▶	65	
	66	Estimated tax penalty (see page 33). Also include on line 65 66		

Sign Here

Keep a copy of this return for your records.

Under penalties of perjury, I declare that I have examined this return and accompanying schedules and statements, and to the best of my knowledge and belief, they are true, correct, and complete. Declaration of preparer (other than taxpayer) is based on all information of which preparer has any knowledge.

▶ Your signature	Date	Your occupation
▶ Spouse's signature. If a joint return, BOTH must sign.	Date	Spouse's occupation

Paid Preparer's Use Only

Preparer's signature ▶	Date	Check if self-employed ☐	Preparer's social security no.
Firm's name (or yours if self-employed) and address ▶		EIN	
		ZIP code	

1. How do you determine if you get a refund or owe taxes?

   _____

   _____

   _____

2. Use the information on the tax form to determine Juan's refund or the tax he owes. Then check your answers with a partner.

   Partner's name _____

If line 54 is	and	line 61 is,	Refund	or	Tax owed
A. $2,182.00		$1,987.00	_____		_____
B. $895.00		$932.00	_____		_____
C. $4,189.00		$4,198.00	_____		_____

Using a Tax Table

Topic: Finding federal tax on a tax table

1995 Tax Table—*Continued*

If line 37 (taxable income) is—		And you are—				If line 37 (taxable income) is—		And you are—			
At least	But less than	Single	Married filing jointly *	Married filing separately	Head of a household	At least	But less than	Single	Married filing jointly *	Married filing separately	Head of a household
		Your tax is—						Your tax is—			
25,000						**26,000**					
25,000	25,050	3,972	3,754	4,472	3,754	26,000	26,050	4,252	3,904	4,752	3,904
25,050	25,100	3,986	3,761	4,486	3,761	26,050	26,100	4,266	3,911	4,766	3,911
25,100	25,150	4,000	3,769	4,500	3,769	26,100	26,150	4,280	3,919	4,780	3,919
25,150	25,200	4,014	3,776	4,514	3,776	26,150	26,200	4,294	3,926	4,794	3,926
25,200	25,250	4,028	3,784	4,528	3,784	26,200	26,250	4,308	3,934	4,808	3,934
25,250	25,300	4,042	3,791	4,542	3,791	26,250	26,300	4,322	3,941	4,822	3,941
25,300	25,350	4,056	3,799	4,556	3,799	26,300	26,350	4,336	3,949	4,836	3,949
25,350	25,400	4,070	3,806	4,570	3,806	26,350	26,400	4,350	3,956	4,850	3,956
25,400	25,450	4,084	3,814	4,584	3,814	26,400	26,450	4,364	3,964	4,864	3,964
25,450	25,500	4,098	3,821	4,598	3,821	26,450	26,500	4,378	3,971	4,878	3,971
25,500	25,550	4,112	3,829	4,612	3,829	26,500	26,550	4,392	3,979	4,892	3,979
25,550	25,600	4,126	3,836	4,626	3,836	26,550	26,600	4,406	3,986	4,906	3,986
25,600	25,650	4,140	3,844	4,640	3,844	26,600	26,650	4,420	3,994	4,920	3,994
25,650	25,700	4,154	3,851	4,654	3,851	26,650	26,700	4,434	4,001	4,934	4,001
25,700	25,750	4,168	3,859	4,668	3,859	26,700	26,750	4,448	4,009	4,948	4,009
25,750	25,800	4,182	3,866	4,682	3,866	26,750	26,800	4,462	4,016	4,962	4,016
25,800	25,850	4,196	3,874	4,696	3,874	26,800	26,850	4,476	4,024	4,976	4,024
25,850	25,900	4,210	3,881	4,710	3,881	26,850	26,900	4,490	4,031	4,990	4,031
25,900	25,950	4,224	3,889	4,724	3,889	26,900	26,950	4,504	4,039	5,004	4,039
25,950	26,000	4,238	3,896	4,738	3,896	26,950	27,000	4,518	4,046	5,018	4,046

Use the Tax Table to find the tax for each person.

1. Lin's taxable income is $26,582.00. She filed SINGLE.

   Her tax is $ _____

2. Satish's taxable income is $25,122.00. He filed SINGLE.

   His tax is $ _____

3. The Cho's taxable income is $25,954.00. They filed JOINTLY.

   Their tax is $ _____

4. Paula Perry's taxable income is $26,930. She is HEAD OF A HOUSEHOLD.

   Her tax is $ _____.

A Simple Debate

Topics: Rules for a formal debate, ethical dilemmas,
formulating arguments on a topic

A debate is an argument between two sides or teams, one team
agreeing with (defending) a statement (the pros), and the other team
arguing against the argument or attacking it (the cons). Each team has
two members. Each team member speaks in a fixed order and for a
limited amount of time.

> **Presentation order:**
> Pro I: 5-minute (maximum) presentation
> Con I: 5-minute (maximum) presentation
> Pro 2:   5 minutes (maximum) to add more pro arguments and
>   to contradict Con I
> Con 2:   5 minutes (maximum) to add more con arguments and
>   to contradict both Pro I and Pro 2

Then the four team members answer questions from "the floor"
(the entire class).

*Divide the class into two groups, the pros and the cons. Each group
talks among itself and writes down arguments for (or against) the
statement. Then each group picks two people to present (debate) their
position. Pick one of these topics, or decide on an entirely new topic.*

1. The death penalty (known as "capital punishment") should be
   abolished.

2. Physical punishment (such as paddling, flogging, caning, and
   disfiguring) should be used as the proper punishment for a crime.

3. Women are the best persons for the job (or any job).

4. English should be the only language used in the United States for all
   official business: on ballots, on driver's license exams, on tax forms,
   in classrooms, etc.

5. Your own topic: _____

_____

Constitutional Amendments 11–26

Task 1:

Work with a partner. Go to a library and find a copy of the last 16 amendments to the U.S. Constitution. Read them over then answer these questions.

Partner's name _____

1. Which amendment did away with slavery? What year was it passed?

   _____

2. Which amendment gave Congress the right to collect taxes on income? What year was it passed?

   _____

3. Which amendment gave women the right to vote? In what year?

   _____

4. Which amendment repealed the eighteenth amendment? What year?

   _____

5. Which amendment gave citizens eighteen years and older the right to vote? What year was it passed?

   _____

Task 2:

Pick one of these places to visit and report back to the class on.

1. City Hall
2. A courthouse
3. A political campaign headquarters

✔ Summary: Democratic Government Checklist

Check (✓) one.

Yes **No** **Need more practice**

☐ ☐ ☐ I can talk about political parties.
(example: p. 58

☐ ☐ ☐ I can name and describe the three branches of the U.S. government.
(example: p. 54. *"The judicial branch explains and interprets the laws."*)

☐ ☐ ☐ I can name the federal officials from my state and district.
(example: p. 55)

☐ ☐ ☐ I can talk about the Bill of Rights.
(example: p. 56. *"The eighth amendment prohibits cruel and unusual punishment."*)

☐ ☐ ☐ I understand the Miranda Rule and my personal legal rights.
(example: p. 57. *"I have the right to remain silent."*)

☐ ☐ ☐ I can talk about taxes and tax forms.
(example: p. 61. *"Juan's gross income is $28,950."*)

☐ ☐ ☐ I can complete a 1040 tax form.
(example: p. 67.)

☐ ☐ ☐ I have read over the other 16 amendments of the U.S. Constitution.
(example: p. 70.)

Write two other things you can say or do in English.

I can _____ .

I can _____ .

_____
Signature

Teacher's comments: _____

_____

Unit 5 Technology

LANGUAGE FUNCTIONS

On completion, students will have used English for:

▲ factual information: to analyze, to evaluate, to paraphrase, to summarize.
▲ social and interpersonal relations: to express values, to express judgment.

LANGUAGE FORMS

On completion, students will have used the following structures:

▲ **Sentence types**
  Complex sentences
▲ **Verb tenses**
  Continuous conditional

LANGUAGE SKILLS

Listening: On completion, students will have:

▲ demonstrated understanding of conversation in encounters with native speakers with little repetition or rewording.
▲ demonstrated understanding of descriptions and narrations of factual and technical material.

Speaking: On completion, students will have:

▲ spoken fluently in most formal and informal conversations on practical and social topics, except when under tension or pressure.
▲ spoken with some fluency on technical subjects or on special fields of interest related to academic pursuits or work demands.

Reading: On completion, students will have:

▲ read authentic printed material and prose on familiar topics.
▲ interpreted main ideas and key points from technical material in their own fields of interest.
▲ applied appropriate reading strategies for understanding content on unfamiliar topics or in technical information.
▲ used syntactic clues to interpret the meaning of complex sentences and new vocabulary.
▲ reacted personally to reading materials by making judgments or by prioritizing values.

Writing: On completion, students will have:

▲ punctuated paragraphs, making only minor errors.
▲ written paragraphs on familiar topics, using the techniques of comparison/contrast, cause/effect, generalization/example, and exposition.
▲ taken notes from lectures.
▲ written summaries of reading passages.

A Computer System

Topics: Components, Input/Output

Look at the illustration and listen to the description of a computer sytem's makeup.

Input/Output

The computer's keyboard, mouse, disk drives, scanner, screen, and printer are all Input/Output (I/O) devices. Because the computer understands and uses only its own binary language, all these devices are needed to communicate with the computer.

Some of these devices, such as the keyboard, mouse, and scanner, are considered to be Input devices. They are used only to put information or data into the computer. A screen and printer are considered Output devices because they display or print out processed information or text.

Disk drives, which can send *or* receive information, and modems, which connect a computer to a telephone line, are both Input and Output devices. The CRT screen is an Output device, but with the development of the touch screen, it can now be used as an Input device as well.

Listen again. With a partner, take turns asking and answering questions about information from entry to the printed copy.

Partner's name _____

Suggested questions:
 What are a computer's Input devices?
 What is the purpose of an Input device?

A Computer System's, Memory

Topics: RAM, ROM, definitions, acronyms

Listen to the description of a computer's memory storage systems.

A computer system has a built-in, or internal, memory and a secondary, or external, memory. The computer's secondary memory refers to the magnetic hard and soft disks (also known as floppies), magnetic back-up tape, and CDs used to store data. These are run on I/O devices and are stored outside the computer.

The computer's internal memory can only "remember" or store data. (*Data* is the plural of *datum* and refers to the actual facts or figures.) The computer has two types of internal memory: Random Access Memory (RAM) and Read Only Memory (ROM).

RAM is the computer's temporary memory. It stores data that the user loads into the system through an Input device such as a keyboard or disk drive. The data stored in RAM is lost every time you turn off the computer. You can transfer the data you put in RAM onto disk or tape to save and store it, but it must be reloaded when you want to use it again. The data in RAM can be added to, changed, or erased by the user. It is the part of the computer that holds the particular or specific data, instructions, and programs that the user is working with.

The computer's other type of internal memory, ROM, is pre-programmed at the factory and stores the permanent instructions for the computer. These instructions cannot be changed or erased. They are the basic instructions that operate every computer.

Listen again. ROM and RAM are acronyms—*words formed from the initial letter(s) of a multiword term.*

Examples: **IBM** = International Business Machines
CPU = Central Processing Unit

Look at the acronyms and write their full equivalents. Then check your work with a partner.

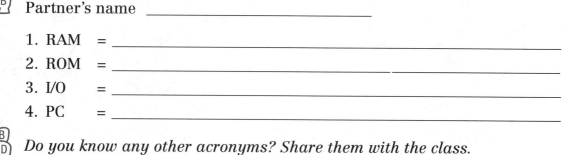

Partner's name _____

1. RAM = _____

2. ROM = _____

3. I/O   = _____

4. PC   = _____

Do you know any other acronyms? Share them with the class.

_____

_____

Practice 21

Choosing a Search Option by Number

In most libraries, computer on-line search devices have replaced card catalogs. Multidrawer setups have been replaced by electronic systems that occupy a fraction of the space formerly occupied by card files. Read the directions.

Library Search
Choose a search option by number.
            1: Author
            2: Title
            3: Subject
            4: Quit searching
Enter a number: ___ and press "Enter"
Commands: SO = Start Over   B = Back   ? = HELP

Screen 1: Choose the type of search you want. For example, if you know the author's name, type in "1" for author and press "Enter."

Author Search
Author: last name, first name
        Example: Buck, Pearl S
Enter author (last name, first): _____
and press "Enter"
Commands: SO = Start Over   B = Back   ? = HELP

Screen 2: Type in the author's last name and then first name; press "Enter." For example, if the author's last name is Buck, type that in and press "Enter."

Your Search: Buck
      Author   Titles
1. Buck, Pearl S   73
2. Buck, Peter   1
3. Buck, Polly   1
Enter a line number for more detail: ___ and press "Enter"
Commands: SO = Start Over   B = Back   ? = HELP

Screen 3: Enter the line number of the author you want. For example, if you want a book by Pearl S. Buck, enter "1."

Your Search: Buck, Pearl S.
      Author   Date
1. Buck, Pearl S.   1932
    Sons
2. Buck, Pearl S.
    The Good Earth   1931
3. Buck, Pearl S.
    Imperial Woman   1956
Enter a line number for more detail or press "A" for more titles: ___ and press "Enter"
Commands: SO = Start Over   B = Back   ? = HELP

Screen 4: Type in the line number for the title you're looking for and press "Enter." For example, if the book you're looking for is *The Good Earth*, type in "2" and press "Enter."

Author: Buck, Pearl S.
Title: The Good Earth
Publisher: Harper and Row
Call Number: FB92251
Number of Copies: 18
Status: Available
Commands: SO = Start Over   B = Back
           Return = Next Screen

Screen 5: This is the listing for *The Good Earth* by Pearl S. Buck.

Follow the directions to complete the entry on each screen.

A Time Line of Scientific Advances

Scene
22

Topics: Scientific advances, developing technology through the centuries

Pascal invents the first mechanical adding machine.

John Atanasoff invents the first electronic digital computer.

John Glenn is the first American to orbit the earth in space.

Herman Hollerith invents the tabulating machine. Automated data processing is born.

Neil Armstrong is the first man to land on the moon.

3000 BC   1801   1903   1952   1967   1995

1642   1880   1942   1961   1969

Jacquard invents a loom controlled by punch-cards.

Jonas Salk discovers the polio vaccine.

Abacus is developed by the Chinese.

Dr. Christian Barnard performs the first sucessful human heart transplant.

The Wright Brothers achieve the first powered flight.

U.S. and Russia establish the first joint venture space station.

Look at the historical time line of scientific advances. Then match the event with the science it influenced the most.

Medicine	Computer	Engineering (Aerospace)
_____	_____	_____
_____	_____	_____
_____	_____	_____
_____	_____	_____

Practice
22

Describing a Time Line

Topics: Paragraph writing, essay organization

Go to a library and look up information on one of the sciences mentioned on page 77 or on another science of your choice. Construct a time line of the events, listed or unlisted, that led up to a particular scientific advance or breakthrough. From your notes write a three-to five-paragraph essay. Include a final copy of your time line.

_____

_____

_____

_____

_____

_____

_____

_____

_____

_____

_____

_____

_____

_____

_____

_____

_____

_____

_____

_____

_____

_____

_____

_____

_____

_____

An Oral Presentation of a Technical Topic

Topics: Researching, note-taking, oral presentation

Pick one of the sciences you know about, work with, or are interested in. Prepare a 3 to 5 minute oral presentation for the class. Use the space to write an outline of your presentation. Then give your presentation to the class. Try to use the notes as memory-joggers only; do not read from them.

_____

_____

_____

_____

_____

_____

_____

_____

_____

_____

_____

_____

_____

_____

_____

_____

_____

_____

_____

_____

_____

_____

_____

_____

Evaluating Oral Technical Presentations

Practice 23

Topic: **Using value judgments, figuring averages**

Use the evaluation forms to evaluate your classmates's presentations on technical subjects.

ORAL PRESENTATION EVALUATION

Presenter's name _____   Topic/Title _____

| 1 = Poor | 2 = Needs improvement | 3 = Good | 4 = Excellent |

Circle one:

Pronunciation (easy to understand)	1	2	3	4
Fluency (easy to follow)	1	2	3	4
Usage (grammar/structure)	1	2	3	4
Preparation (well thought-out)	1	2	3	4
Knowledge of material	1	2	3	4
Overall presentation	1	2	3	4

Total score (add all the scores) _____   Average score (total score divided by 6) _____

Comments _____

_____

ORAL PRESENTATION EVALUATION

Presenter's name _____   Topic/Title _____

| 1 = Poor | 2 = Needs improvement | 3 = Good | 4 = Excellent |

Circle one:

Pronunciation (easy to understand)	1	2	3	4
Fluency (easy to follow)	1	2	3	4
Usage (grammar/structure)	1	2	3	4
Preparation (well thought-out)	1	2	3	4
Knowledge of material	1	2	3	4
Overall presentation	1	2	3	4

Total score (add all the scores) _____   Average score (total score divided by 6) _____

Comments _____

_____

ORAL PRESENTATION EVALUATION

Presenter's name _____   Topic/Title _____

| 1 = Poor | 2 = Needs improvement | 3 = Good | 4 = Excellent |

Circle one:

Pronunciation (easy to understand)	1	2	3	4
Fluency (easy to follow)	1	2	3	4
Usage (grammar/structure)	1	2	3	4
Preparation (well thought-out)	1	2	3	4
Knowledge of material	1	2	3	4
Overall presentation	1	2	3	4

Total score (add all the scores) _____   Average score (total score divided by 6) _____

Comments _____

_____

Lifeskills/ Workskills

4

Continuous Conditional Sentences

Topics: Grammar skills: Present continuous conditional, future continuous conditional

In a conditional sentence, the continuous form of the verb is used to show action or progression. The conditional sentence is made up of:

an *if* clause   +   a result clause

In the present continuous conditional:
an *if*   +   present continuous   +   a result clause

Example: If you are sleeping, I'm going to the store.

In the future continuous conditional:

if   +   future continuous   +   result clause

Example: If you are going to tell him, I'm going to go home.

Complete the conditional sentences. Then check your answers with a partner.

Partner's name _____

1. If you aren't using the hammer, I _____
   (use)

   _____ it.

2. If we _____, don't wake us.
   (sleep)

3. If they are going to be there, we aren't _____
   (go)

   _____.

4. If I am going to visit the United States, I'm _____
   (study)

   _____ English.

5. If he is working, we are not _____
   (bother)

   _____ him.

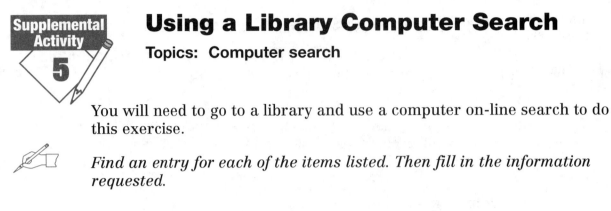

Using a Library Computer Search

Topics: Computer search

You will need to go to a library and use a computer on-line search to do this exercise.

Find an entry for each of the items listed. Then fill in the information requested.

1. A novel by Ernest Hemingway.

   _____
   title   call number   availability

2. A play by Ibsen.

   _____
   title   call number   availability

3. A collection of modern American short stories.

   _____
   title   call number   availability

4. A book about the history of baseball.

   _____
   title   author   availability

5. *To Kill a Mockingbird.*

   _____
   author   call number   availability

6. A poem by Carl Sandberg.

   _____
   title of collection   title of poem

7. Information about the discovery of electricity.

   _____
   title   author   availability

8. Impressionist artists and styles

   _____
   title   author

9. a vegetarian cookbook

   _____
   title   publisher   date

☑ Summary: Technology Checklist

Check (✓) one.

**Yes   No   Need
              more
              practice**

☐ ☐ ☐ I can describe a computer system.
         (example: pp. 74 and 75. (*"A screen and printer are
         Output devices."*)

☐ ☐ ☐ I can explain and form acronyms.
         (example: p. 75)

☐ ☐ ☐ I can use a computer to search in a library catalog.
         (example: p. 76)

☐ ☐ ☐ I can talk about scientific advances.
         (example: p. 77)

☐ ☐ ☐ I can give a three- to five-minute technical presentation
         (example: p. 79)

☐ ☐ ☐ I can evaluate a technical presentation.
         (example: p. 80)

☐ ☐ ☐ I can write a continous conditional sentence.
         (example: p. 81)

Write two other things you can say or do in English.

I can _____ .

I can _____ .

_____
Signature

Teacher's comments: _____

_____

Time Zones in the Continental United States

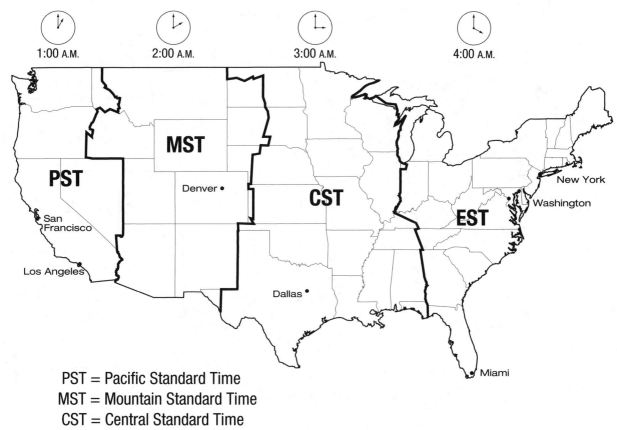

PST = Pacific Standard Time
MST = Mountain Standard Time
CST = Central Standard Time
EST = Eastern Standard Time

U.S. Map

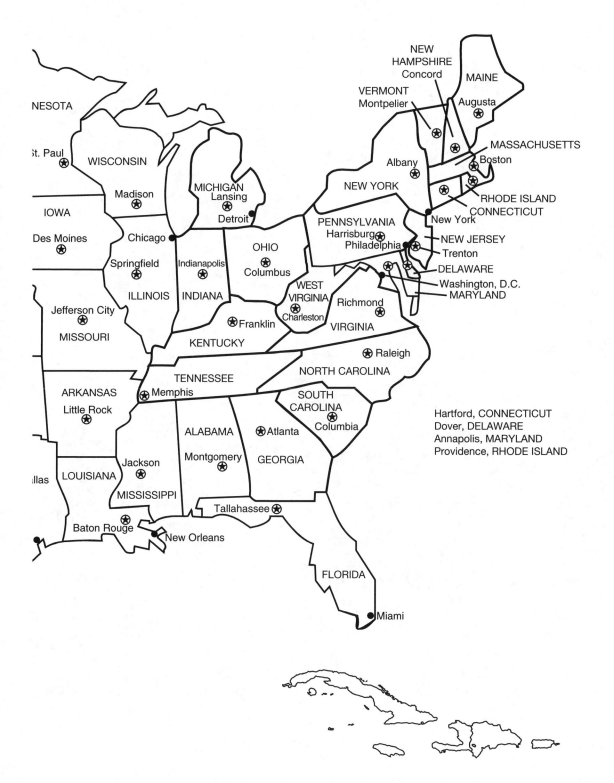

NEW
HAMPSHIRE
Concord
VERMONT   MAINE
Montpelier   Augusta

MASSACHUSETTS
Albany   Boston
NEW YORK   RHODE ISLAND
CONNECTICUT

NESOTA
St. Paul
WISCONSIN
Madison
MICHIGAN
Lansing
IOWA
Detroit
Des Moines
Chicago
OHIO
PENNSYLVANIA
Harrisburg
Philadelphia
New York
NEW JERSEY
Trenton
DELAWARE
Washington, D.C.
MARYLAND
Springfield
Indianapolis
Columbus
ILLINOIS   INDIANA
WEST
VIRGINIA
Richmond
Jefferson City
Franklin
Charleston
VIRGINIA
MISSOURI
KENTUCKY
Raleigh
NORTH CAROLINA
TENNESSEE
ARKANSAS   Memphis
SOUTH
CAROLINA
Little Rock
Columbia
ALABAMA   Atlanta
Hartford, CONNECTICUT
Dover, DELAWARE
Annapolis, MARYLAND
Providence, RHODE ISLAND
llas LOUISIANA
Jackson
Montgomery   GEORGIA
MISSISSIPPI
Tallahassee
Baton Rouge
New Orleans
FLORIDA
Miami

World Map

World Map

Standard U.S. Units of Measure

Length (Distance)
1 foot (ft) = 12 inches (in.)
1 yard (yd) = 3 ft = 36 in.
1 mile (mi) = 5280 ft = 1760 yd

Time
1 minute (min) = 60 seconds (sec)
1 hour (hr) = 60 min
1 day (da) = 24 hr
1 week (wk) = 7 days
1 year (yr) = 365 days = 12 months (mo) = 52 weeks

Weight
1 pound (lb) = 16 ounces (oz)
1 ton (t) = 2000 lb

Liquid Measure (Volume)
1 cup = 8 oz
1 pint = 2 cup = 16 oz
1 quart (qt) = 2 pt = 32 oz
1 gallon (gal) = 4 qt

Common Metric Measurements

Length (Distance)
1 meter = 1000 millimeters (mm)
1 meter = 100 centimeters (cm)
1 meter = 10 decimeters (dm)
1 kilometer (km) = 1000 meters (m)

Weight
1 gram (g) = 1000 milligrams (mg)
1 gram = 100 centigrams (cg)
1 kilogram (kg) = 1000 grams (g)

Liquid Measure (Volume)
1 liter (l) = 1000 milliliters (ml)
1 liter = 100 centiliters (cl)
1 liter = 10 deciliters (dl)

Common Equivalents

U.S.		**Metric**
Length (Distance)		
1 inch (1 in.)	=	2.5 centimeters (2.5 cm)
1 foot (1 ft)	=	30 centimeters (30 cm)
1 yard (1 yd)	=	0.91 meters (0.91 m)
1 mile (1 mi)	=	1.6 kilometers (1.6 km)
or		
0.4 inch (4/10 in.)	=	1 centimeter (1 cm)
1.1 yards (1 1/10 yd)	=	1 meter (1 m)
0.62 miles (6/10 mi)	=	1 kilometer (1 km)
Weight		
1 ounce (1 oz)	=	28 grams (28 g)
1 pound (1 lb)	=	0.4 kilogram (0.4 kg)
or		
2.2 pounds (2 2/10 lb)	=	1 kilogram (1 kg)
Liquid Measure (Volume)		
1 fluid ounce (1 fl oz)	=	29.5 milliliters (29.5 ml)
1 quart (1 qt)	=	0.9 liters (0.9 l)
or		
1.05 quarts (1 5/100 qt)	=	1 liter (1 l)

Temperature: Fahrenheit and Celsius

Fahrenheit   **Celsius**

212°F = 100°C (boiling point)

100°F =   38°C

32°F   =   0°C (freezing point)

0°F   = −18°CT

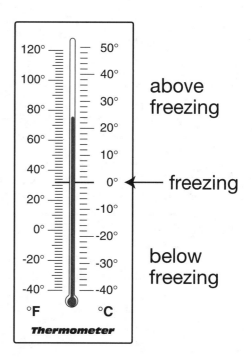

120° — 50°

100° — 40°

80° — 30°

— 20°

60° — 10°

40° —

20° — 0°   ← freezing

— -10°

0° — -20°

-20° — -30°

-40° — -40°

°F   °C

Thermometer

above
freezing

below
freezing

To change **Fahrenheit** to **Celsius**:

Example

1. Start with Fahrenheit degrees.   86° Fahrenheit
2. Subtract 32.   86 − 32 = 54
3. Multiply the answer by 5/9.   54 x 5/9 = 30°

   86° Fahrenheit = 30° Celsius

To change **Celsius** to **Fahrenheit**:

Example

1. Start with Celsius degrees.   10° Celsius
2. Divide Celsius by 5/9.   10 ÷ 5/9 = 18
3. Add 32 to the answer   18 + 32 = 50°

   10° Celsius = 50° Fahrenheit

A shortcut method to find approximate equivalencies

To change Celsius to Fahrenheit, double the
Celsius number and add 30.

To change Fahrenheit to Celsius, subtract 30
from the Fahrenheit and divide by 2.

Useful Words and Expressions

Irregular Verbs

be	was/were	been
begin	began	begun
bend	bent	bent
bite	bit	bitten
blow	blew	blown
break	broke	broken
bring	brought	brought
build	built	built
buy	bought	bought
catch	caught	caught
choose	chose	chosen
come	came	come
cost	cost	cost
cut	cut	cut
dig	dug	dug
do	did	done
draw	drew	drawn
drink	drank	drunk
drive	drove	driven
eat	ate	eaten
fall	fell	fallen
feed	fed	fed
feel	felt	felt
fight	fought	fought
find	found	found
fly	flew	flown
forget	forgot	forgotten
get	got	gotten
give	gave	given
go	went	gone
grow	grew	grown
hang	hung	hung
have	had	had
hear	heard	heard
hide	hid	hidden
hit	hit	hit
hold	held	held
hurt	hurt	hurt
keep	kept	kept
know	knew	known
leave	left	left

Irregular Verbs

lend	lent	lent
let	let	let
lose	lost	lost
make	made	made
mean	meant	meant
meet	met	met
pay	paid	paid
put	put	put
quit	quit	quit
read	read	read
ride	rode	ridden
ring	rang	rung
run	ran	run
say	said	said
see	saw	seen
seek	sought	sought
sell	sold	sold
send	sent	sent
set	set	set
shake	shook	shaken
show	showed	shown
shut	shut	shut
sing	sang	sung
sit	sat	sat
sleep	slept	slept
speak	spoke	spoken
spend	spent	spent
stand	stood	stood
sweep	swept	swept
swim	swam	swum
take	took	taken
teach	taught	taught
tear	tore	torn
tell	told	told
think	thought	thought
throw	threw	thrown
understand	understood	understood
wake	woke	woken
wear	wore	worn
win	won	won
write	wrote	written

Common Abbreviations: Spoken and Written

AAA (Triple A)	American Automobile Association
AC	Alternating current
AIDS	Acquired Immune Deficiency Syndrome
A.M.	*Ante meridiem* morning (before noon)
A–one or A1	First class, excellent
ASAP	As soon as possible
B.A.	Bachelor of Arts degree
CD	Certificate of deposit; Compact disk
CEO	Chief executive officer
DC	Direct current; District of Columbia
DDS	Doctor of Dental Science
DMV	Department of Motor Vehicles
FBI	Federal Bureau of Investigation
HBO	Home Box Office
ID	Identification card
IOU	I owe you.
IRS	Internal Revenue Service
M.A.	Master of Arts degree
MD	Doctor of Medicine (*Medicinae Doctor*)
NASA	National Aeronautics and Space Administration
Ph.D.	Doctor of Philosophy degree
P.M.	*Post meridiem* (after noon)
PO	Post Office
P.S.	Postscript; Public School; Police Sergeant
PTA or PTO	Parent-Teacher Association (or Organization)
Rev.	Revised; Reverend
Prof.	Professor
RN	Registered nurse
RSVP	Please reply (*Respondez, s'il vous plait*)
TV	television
TGIF	Thank God it's Friday!
UFO	Unidentified flying object
UK	United Kingdom
UNESCO	United Nations Educational, Scientific, and Cultural Organization
UNICEF	United Nations Children's Fund
VIP	Very important person
VP	Vice president
WHO	World Health Organization
YMCA/YWCA	Young Men's Christian Association, Young Women's Christian Association

Certificate of Completion

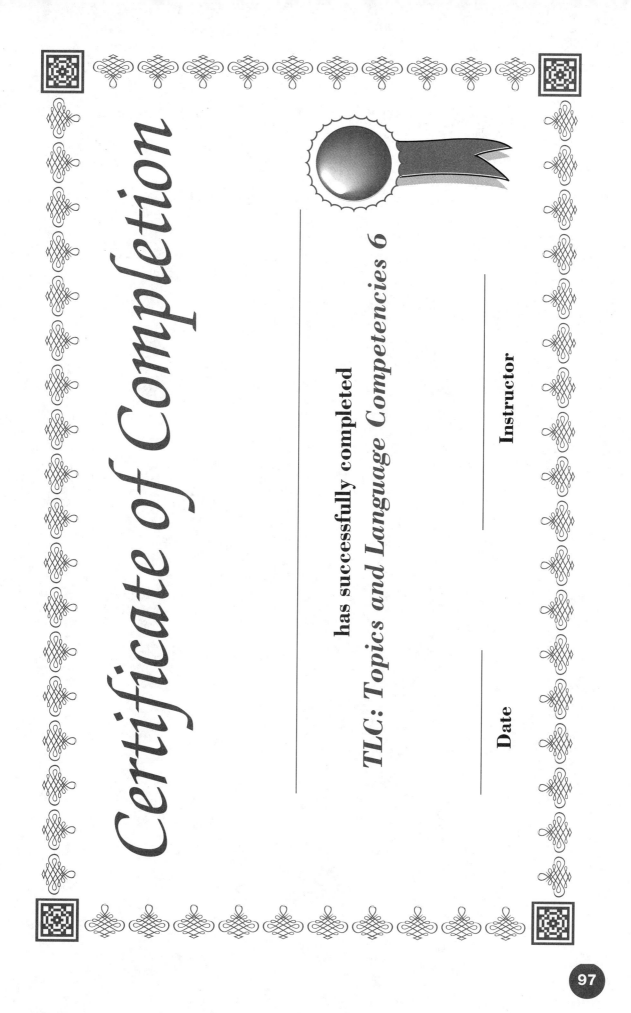

has successfully completed

TLC: Topics and Language Competencies 6

_____
Instructor

_____
Date